PLA

AROUND

THE

BASES

A Historic Tour
of the
Coors Field Neighborhood

WRITTEN BY
DIANE BAKKE AND JACKIE DAVIS

PUBLISHED BY
WESTCLIFFE PUBLISHERS, INC.
ENGLEWOOD, COLORADO

International Standard Book Number: 1-56579-117-7
Library of Congress catalog Number: 94-62205
Text © 1995 Diane Bakke and Jackie Davis
Publisher: John Fielder
Project Manager: Suzanne Venino
Editor: Dougald MacDonald
Designer: Nancy V. Rice, Nancy Rice Graphic Design
Indexer: Doug Easton, New West Indexing

Published by
Westcliffe Publishers, Inc.
2650 South Zuni Street
Englewood, CO 80110

Printed in Michigan by BookCrafters

Cover Photos:
Union Station — Randy Brown Photographer
Coors Field under construction — Emmett Jordan/Rich Clarkson
    & Associates
Denver's first professional baseball team, The Denvers — Jay Sanford
    collection
Lower downtown street sign — Randy Brown Photographer

A C K N O W L E D G E M E N T S

As with all similar endeavors, this book was written with help from a great many generous people, who opened their hearts and their files and shared their memories with us.

We could not have written this book without the assistance of Jay Sanford, baseball historian, who proofread our first two sections and kept us on the right track. Roger Kinney from the Colorado Rockies Baseball Club, Gary Jones from Mile High Stadium, Bob Howsam, Frank Haraway, Dave Garland, Jr., and Clint Bowman also added much to these sections with their first-hand knowledge of the baseball events that took place in Denver.

We also owe thanks to Stewart Ervie, J. Bradley Schrock, and Vanda Meehan from Hellmuth, Obata & Kassabaum, Inc.; Chuck and Kathy Simmons, Moe Mahon, Bill Bell, and Guy Prochilo from Mortenson/Barton Malow JV; John Lehigh and Lynnette Booker from the Denver Metropolitan Major League Baseball Stadium District; Emmett Jordan and Nate Cox from Rich Clarkson & Associates; and Joshua Hassel and the artists Jeff Starr, Matt O'Neill, Lonnie Hanzon, and Erick Johnson. Jerry McMorris, Jennifer Moore, Jimmy Oldham, and John Kehl from the Colorado Rockies were most generous in acquainting us with the new Coors Field and sharing photographs of its growth with us, and thanks also are owed to Peter Coors and Steve Saunders of Coors Brewing Company.

Sharing their own or their families' experiences with us for a historic look at the Coors Field neighborhood were Miyuki Mabel Googins, director of Tamai Towers; Father Marcus Medrano of Sacred Heart Church; the Reverend Kanya Okamoto, minister of the Tri-State Buddhist Temple; Ed and Helen Maestas of Johnnie's Market on Larimer Street; Sadako and Willie Hasegawa; Karle Seydel, AICP, executive director of the Ball Park Neighborhood; Norma L. Mumey, widow of historian Dr. Nolie Mumey; Rick Borman, developer; Martin

Murphy and George Stevens of Murphy Stevens architects; Max Silverman of Maximilian's; Stephen Cowperthwaite; M. J. Baum; Hank Bowes; Nancy Mitchell; Royal Judd; James Judd; Art Judd; Manny Salzman; Joann Salzman; and Naomi Salzman.

In addition, we received help from David Gottlieb, past director of Lower Downtown District Inc.; David Herlinger from the Colorado Housing and Finance Authority; Teri Whelan from Senior Housing Options, Inc.; Bob Seifort from Kuner Empson Company; Rita MacEllaio from the Chicago Board of Trade; David Stivers from Nabisco Food Group; Bill Strubel and Dan Ferguson from Meadow Gold Dairy; Dan Murphy of Americold: James Lankin, Marilyn Hillius, and Ray Bissell from Timpte Industries Inc.; Jerry Baker and Kenton Forrest, railroad historians; Richard W. McSpadden, general manager of the Denver Union Terminal Railway Co., and Betty Tideball with Union Station; Bill Katville and Don Snoddy from Union Pacific Railroad Co.; Mike McNeill, public information officer with the Denver Fire Department; Jerry Krantz and Lupe Ashley from El Chapultepec; Donna Casillas from La Casa de Manuel; and Dana Crawford and John Hinkenlooper, developers who have owned or own businesses in the area. Also, thanks to Barbara Wetzel and Mr. and Mrs. George Cannon.

Digging through archives, libraries, historical photographs, newspapers, maps, and directories was made much easier with the help of the wonderful staff at the Western History Library, including Bruce Hanson, Lisa Buckman, Don Dilley, Cathy Swan, and Phil Panum, along with Jeanne Conway and Mary Sullivan and the preservation office of the Colorado Historical Society and Jim Parker at the State Archives. Thanks also to the folks on the second floor of Colorado Historical Society: Peg Ekstrand, David Wetzel, Stan Olinger, Barbara Foley, Jean Settles, Becky Lintz, David Hallas, Clark Secrest, Eric Paddock, and Jennifer Bosley. And thanks to David Becker at the city planning office and Phil Cummings, staff engineer for the city and county of Denver. Also, thank you to Maggie Kelly of the Chicago Historical Society for her assistance. Thanks also to architect Kenneth Fuller and historian Tom Noel, the archivists at the Burlington Northern Railway Co. in Fort Worth, Texas, the Newberry Library in Chicago, and Kathleen Brooker of Historic Denver.

We appreciate the hard work of our editors, Dougald MacDonald and Suzanne Venino, as well as our designer, Nancy Rice, and our photographer, Randy Brown. Thanks also to Dianne Howie and John Fielder for the faith they had in our project.

Finally, we owe thanks to our husbands, Jerry Bakke and Lou Davis, families, and friends, who put up with us for almost two years while we researched and wrote this book, and to Dotty Gerard who painstakingly typed our drafts. We want to thank all of the people above for their infinite patience and help.

The Colorado Rockies brought new excitement with major-league baseball to the Rocky Mountain region. Coors Field, the Rockies' new home, has brought new energy and vitality to one of Denver's oldest neighborhoods. This is a community rich in history and tradition. We hope you enjoy exploring it as much as we do.

Diane Bakke
Jackie Davis

TABLE OF CONTENTS

BASEBALL IN DENVER
*FROM MOUNTAIN MEN
TO MAJOR LEAGUERS*

"The world will little note, nor long remember, what happened here yesterday, but the Colorado Rockies never can forget what they did here. They got a life."

— Woody Paige
The Denver Post, April 6, 1993

One hundred and seven years after the first professional baseball team played in Denver, baseball fans' dream finally came true on April 5, 1993, as the Colorado Rockies played their first major-league game. This event marked the end of Denver's long road to a major-league franchise, and it was received with great enthusiasm around the whole Rocky Mountain region. Fans from 37 states and foreign countries bought an amazing 28,627 season tickets in the first year, and the Rockies set a single-season attendance record of 4,483,350 spectators.

Baseball, or games like it, has a long tradition in Colorado, in the country, and in the world. A ball-and-stick game called rounders was played as early as the seventeenth century. The 1744 book of poetry *A Little Pretty Pocketbook*, by an unknown author, contains this verse:

> *B is fo*
> *Base ball*
> *The ball once struck off*
> *Away flies the boy*
> *To the next destined post*
> *And then home with joy*

An early form of baseball was played by Revolutionary War soldiers in their free time, and Jane Austen mentions a game of base ball in her 1796 book Northanger Abbey. Baseball as it is known today evolved from the many variations of the game played throughout America, such as cricket, rounders, goal ball, and town ball. Over the years, clubs in different regions developed their own style of play and rules.

Abner Doubleday is often credited with inventing the modern form of baseball at Cooperstown, New York, in 1839. This conclusion is based largely on testimony by Abner Graves, a mining engineer and real estate developer from Denver who said he had gone to school with Doubleday in Cooperstown that year and recalled seeing him organize a baseball game. But Doubleday was at West Point, not Cooperstown, in 1839, and he never claimed to have created the game.

Instead, most baseball historians now say Alexander Joy Cartwright, Jr. was the "Father of Baseball." As with many of the young men of his day, Cartwright played early forms of baseball. It was the perfect game for the time because little training or equipment was needed and games could be played on rough fields. Cartwright was part of a group that organized the Knickerbockers Base Ball Club in New York City in 1845. Because there were so many different rules and styles of fields in use, Cartwright took it upon himself in 1846 to establish the rules that became the forerunner for baseball today. Among them were the diamond-shaped infield with bases set at 42-pace intervals, a pitcher 45 feet from home plate, foul lines, nine players to a team, and an umpire who could call strikes and balls.

The early clubs like the Knickerbockers were organized by wealthy young gentlemen who kept the manners and sportsmanship of the game of cricket that they had played prior to baseball. Fines were levied for infractions such as arguing with the umpire, using cuss words, or disobeying the team captain. The sport's gentility was exemplified in the gala dinners hosted by the home team after the game. Spectators attended the games by invitation only, and in some instances tents were erected as protection from the elements, and tea and biscuits and other light refreshments were served.

Cartwright left New York in 1849 to join the gold seekers in California. In *Primitive Baseball*, Harvey Frommer quotes from Cartwright's diary notes of April 23, 1849: "During the past week we have passed the time fixing wagon covers, stowing property, etc., varied by hunting, fishing and playing base ball. It is comical to see the mountain men and Indians playing the new game. I have the ball with me that we used back home."

◆ EARLY TERMS OF THE GAME ◆

EARLY TERM	MODERN EQUIVALENT
Aces	Runs
Bowler	Pitcher
Cranks	Fans
Hand	Out
Hands	Innings
Hippodroming	Fixing games or scores
Kicker	Argument with an umpire
Plugging	Retiring a runner by hitting him with the ball
Revolving	Players selling services to the highest bidder
Soaking or Stinging	Throwing the ball at a runner
Striker	Batter

This is just one instance of how the game spread through the country — geographically as well as across class lines — as the frontier opened. This phenomenon was repeated again when gold was discovered in Colorado. The promise of a new life and new opportunities brought a rush of people from both coasts and the heartland to Colorado, and they brought baseball with them. In 1858, the same year Denver was founded, the National Association of Baseball was formed and went on to formalize the game's regulations and equipment, based largely on Cartwright's rules. Within a few years there were more than 60 clubs, mostly in the East and Midwest. The South lacked National Association clubs, mainly because of Civil War hostilities.

After the first gold was played out in Denver, the city served mainly as a supply town to ranching, farming, and mining communities. But the founding fathers wanted to make their town equal to any city back east. They acquired key water rights and linked Denver to the transcontinental railroad by establishing the Denver Pacific Railroad line to Cheyenne, Wyoming. Baseball was part of the plan, too. In his Civil War History of Colorado, Duane Smith quotes William Byers, publisher of the Rocky

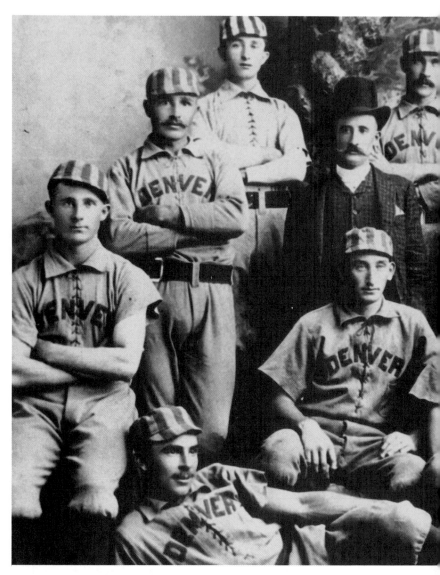

Denver's first professional baseball team, winner of the 1886 Western League pennant. The Denvers' uniforms were "old gold" with red letters, stockings, belts, and stripes on the caps. A young George Tebeau, cofounder of the American

League, is reclining on the right. Darby O'Brian (reclining on left) and Jack Ryan (top row right) co-owned Ball Park Bar on 17th Street, proving that sports bars are not just a recent phenomena. — *Jay Sanford collection*

Base Ball	Massachusetts Ball	Tag Ball
Baste Ball	One Old Cat	Town Ball
Cricket	Paddle Ball	Trap Ball
Goal Ball	Rounders	Two Ol' Cat

Mountain News, stating that baseball was "becoming the National game of America....There is no reason why we here out in this 'neck of the woods'...should be behind our eastern brethren in anything much less in athletic sports."

In 1862, Byers put out a call in the Rocky Mountain News for organized baseball in Denver: "All those wishing to join a base ball club to play according to the rules of modern or New York games will please meet this evening at Whipple's cabinet shop...to effect a permanent organization."

Over the next two decades, amateur and semi-pro teams came and went in Denver. Players sometimes received monetary rewards, but usually the only players paid were the catcher and pitcher. Denver, because of its mining economy, was one of the few towns where players were showered with gold nuggets and coins for exceptional play. Denver secured its first fully salaried team for the 1885 season. Beginning with the 1885 team, Denver baseball clubs produced many fine players. By 1900, according to baseball historian Jay Sanford, Denver had sent at least 20 local players into the big leagues.

But baseball's growth in Denver and its evolution into America's national pastime was not always smooth. The fortunes of the sport waxed and waned depending on economic trends, gold and silver strikes, wars, the quality of the teams, and fans' reactions to the corrupt practices of some players and teams. An old-timer quoted in the Rocky Mountain News explained one dip in the game's popularity this way: "When the game was a comparatively new one, immense crowds attended and...expert

DALRYMPLE, L. F., Denvers

COPYRIGHT BY GOODWIN & CO. 1888

OLD JUDGE
CIGARETTE FACTORY
GOODWIN & CO., New York.

L. F. Dalrymple, a Denvers outfielder. Even in 1888, players were promoting products, as shown on this early baseball card. — *Denver Public Library, Western History Department*

professionals were said to receive salaries amounting in some instances to $8,000 and $10,000 per annum, and this for only about five or six months work in the year with only perhaps three games in the week. This large pay for so little work naturally attracted to the ranks of the players many men who were absolutely devoid of character or principle...[With] several large games having been proven to have been dishonestly played...the proper and natural result [was that a] large number who had previously admired the game for its fairness became disgusted." Mark Twain, an ardent baseball fan whose favorite team was the Hartford Blue Sox, said baseball was "the very symbol, the outward and visible expression of the drive and push and rush and struggle of the raging, tearing, booming nineteenth century."

As early as 1869, the sport had reached a point where fans were willing to support professional teams, beginning with the Cincinnati Red Stockings, baseball's first all-salaried team. This led to a schism between amateur and professional teams, which culminated in the establishment of a professional league, the National Association of Professional Base Ball Players, in 1871.

This league lasted five seasons and gave the players a large voice in management, contracts, and salaries. The league's popularity

Denver Law School Champions, 1898. — *Denver Public Library, Western History Department*

◆ RULE CHANGES ON THE ROAD TO MODERN BASEBALL ◆

William Byers, editor of the Rocky Mountain News, wrote in 1867 that "base ball has become the American National sport.... From year to year the National Convention has met and amended the rules and practice of the game until ball playing is now reduced to an exact science." Byers was a bit premature in calling baseball an "exact science," as the game has continued to evolve until today. Some of the more interesting early changes are listed here.

1845	No soaking or plugging. A player can no longer be put out by having a ball thrown at him while running the bases.
	Pitcher must throw underhanded.
	Batter can request the pitcher to throw high or low.
1865	Fair ball caught on the first bounce no longer equals an out.
1872	Damaged balls can only be changed by an umpire at the end of a complete inning.
1874	Strike zone established. Nine balls equal a walk.
1877	Home plate moves to the position it occupies today, outside the base lines.
1879	Official ball adopted by the National League. First ones manufactured by Albert Spaulding, which is still a major name in sporting goods. Spaulding also wrote the first official baseball guidebook; it was for the National League.
1880	Eight balls equal a walk.
	Pitcher's mound designed by John Montgomery "Monte" Ward, a pitcher for the Providence, Rhode Island, National League team at the time. Ward later went on to play for the New York Giants and formed a players' union, the Brotherhood of Professional Baseball Players.
1881	Seven balls equal a walk
1885	New rules allow overhand delivery by pitchers.
1887	Four strikes equal an out.
	Batter may take first base if struck by ball.
	Batter cannot request high or low pitch.
1888	Three strikes equal an out.
1889	Four balls equal a walk.
1893	Modern pitcher's mound adopted. Pitcher moves back from 50 feet in front of home plate to 60 feet six inches from home plate.

A 1900 team owned by George Tebeau, the first Denver team to be called the Bears, photographed in front of a centerfield billboard at the Athletic Park, or

Base Ball Park, located about where Broadway crosses Cherry Creek. Hall of Famer Joe Tinker is standing second from the left. — *Jay Sanford collection*

The Denver Athletic Club Baseball Team, 1892-1893. The DAC's baseball teams, composed of businessmen who were unable to devote much time to practice, found it became difficult to remain competitive. — *Denver Public Library, Hulbert Western Illustration Collection*

led to expanded newspaper coverage and players who became national heroes. However, it lacked firm schedules, competitive balance, uniform ticket prices, and stability, as teams entered and exited from the league at will.

These factors led W. A. Hulbert to form an eight-team league in 1876, known as the National League of Professional Base Ball Clubs, the forerunner of today's National League. The new league shifted power from players to owners. Membership was limited to well-financed clubs from cities of more than 75,000 people, and each team held monopoly rights to its territory. Hulbert had a strict moral code and insisted that all clubs ban liquor sales, gambling, and Sunday games. In 1879, the owners instituted the reserve clause, which restricted the players' right to switch teams or accept a better salary offer. In many ways, the power of the National League team owners mirrored the monopoly practices of the great business magnates of the period known as the robber barons.

With baseball's growing popularity and financial success, the dominance of the National League inevitably was challenged. From 1882 to 1892, the American Association was a major league that rivaled the National League. But the most significant competition came in 1900 when the Western League's president, Byron "Ban" Johnson, along with Charlie Comiskey and George Tebeau from Denver, restructured the Western League teams into the American League. The American League gained major-league status with the National Agreement of 1903, when the National and American leagues agreed

George "White Wings" Tebeau, founder of the Western League and the American Association, and cofounder of the American League. The roots of organized baseball in Denver — as well as in Kansas City, Missouri, Louisville, Kentucky, and Columbus, Ohio — can be traced to the efforts of this man. — *Jay Sanford collection*

◆ A FEW FIRSTS IN BASEBALL ◆

1867	First curve ball thrown by Brooklyn Excelsiors' Candy Cummings
1869	First all-salaried team, the Cincinnati Red Stockings
1875	First baseball glove worn by Charlie Waitt of the Chicago White Stockings
1880	First night game played, Nantasket Beach, Massachusetts
1883	First Ladies' Day established by Columbus Buckeyes
1884	First rain checks handed out by St. Louis Browns
1905	First All American team selected by and published in Sporting Life.
1908	William Howard Taft is first president to throw out the ball at a season opener

to function separately but as equals. At this point, a recognizable structure of major-league baseball emerged, with a competitive two-league system governed by a commission and a World Series as the annual championship. The first modern World Series was played between the Boston Pilgrims and the Pittsburgh Pirates in 1903; the Pilgrims won five games to three. The agreement also established a better organized and stable minor-league system.

One of the cities that fielded a minor-league team was Denver. George Tebeau, a star player on the 1886 Western League pennant-winning team and also founder of the American Association and cofounder of the American League, was instrumental in securing for the city a minor-league franchise in 1900. Joining the "Denvers" in a reorganized Western League were the Pueblo Indians, the Des Moines Prohibitionists, the Omaha Omahogs

Opposite: Babe Ruth on October 19, 1927, when Ruth's "Bustin' Babes" met Lou Gehrig's "Larrupin' Lous" in an exhibition game at Merchants Park, Broadway and Exposition. This was the year Ruth hit 60 home runs. — *Jay Sanford collection*

Lou Gehrig, batting in an exhibition game at Merchants Park, October 19, 1927. In this game, Gehrig and Babe Ruth each played first base for the opposing

teams. Gehrig won the American League's Most Valuable Player Award that year.
— *Jay Sanford collection*

The Negro All Stars, part of the 1936 Denver Post tournament. The team featured four future Hall of Famers: Satchel Paige (third from left in front row); Josh Gibson

(second from right, front row); Buck Leonard (second from left, middle row); and Cool Papa Bell (fourth from left, middle row). — *Jay Sanford collection*

A Sampling of Team Names, Professional and Amateur

1860s	Colorados, Rocky Mountains, Denver Base Ball Club, Arapahoe Base Ball Club, Young Bachelors Actives, Occidental, Blue Stockings, Unknowns
1870s	Brown Stockings, Clippers, Solis, and Polo's (both cigar brands)
1880s	Blues, Evans & Littlefield, Moreys, McCook, Howards, Blue Labels, Bockfingers, Five Points, Rockets, Prides, Stars, Zacatecas, Maroons, Denver Base Ball and Athletic Club
1900s	Bears, Denvers, Grizzlies, Cubs, Teddy Bears, Denver Skyscrapers, Zangs, Fireclays, Elyrias, Neefs, South Denver Colt, McLaughlins, Dry Climate, Five Points, Tramway, Boulevards, Franklin, Emmanuals, Stickney Cigars, Unions
1984	Denver Zephyrs
1993	Colorado Rockies

(also known as Prairie Sweepers), St. Joseph Saints, and the Sioux City Sioux.

Denver's minor-league team would play off and on for the next 93 years, interrupted mainly by wars and economic depression. In the early years, the team went by various names: the Denvers, Grizzlies, Cubs, or, in deference to Teddy Roosevelt, the Teddy Bears. Eventually, the team became known to everyone as the Bears. Interest in baseball remained high in Denver until after the 1917 season when the Bears stopped playing until 1921 because of World War I.

The early twentieth century brought many nationally known players to Denver, through league games, barnstorming tours in the 1920s, and the annual Denver Post tournaments of the

◆ NATIONAL LEAGUE TEAMS, 1876 ◆

Boston Red Caps	Louisville Grays
Chicago White Stockings	New York Mutuals
Cincinnati Red Stockings	Philadelphia Athletics
Hartford Dark Blues	St. Louis Brown Stockings

1930s and 1940s. Among the standouts were Hall of Famers Joe Tinker, who played for the Denver Skyscrapers and the Chicago Cubs, and Babe Ruth, who played with the local Milliken Whizbangs against the Denver All Stars in 1922 and returned in 1927 to play for the Piggly Wigglys against Lou Gehrig and the Denver Buicks. This was a great year for Denver fans to see these stars in action. Lou Gehrig was named the American League's Most Valuable Player in 1927, and Babe Ruth set a new record with 60 home runs.

In 1922, following World War I, a Bears team returned to play as a Class A minor-league franchise. The team was purchased in 1923 by Milton Anfenger, who retained ownership until 1932 when the Depression forced teams in the Western League to cut travel expenses and the Bears were dropped from the schedule.

During the Depression and World War II, the major focus of baseball in Denver was the semi-pro Denver Post Tournament games. These tournaments brought many famous players to town, including Rogers Hornsby, Satchel Paige, Bob Griffith, Chet Brewer, Josh Gibson, Cool Papa Bell, and Leroy Matlock. The tournament was also notable because it hosted integrated competition in 1934, when Oliver "The Ghost" Marcelle and Poss Parsons, a Denver sportswriter, brought the Kansas City Monarchs, a team of black players, to Denver.

Whether the Denver area had a professional team, a semi-pro team, or no team at all, local enthusiasm for baseball was maintained by amateur competition and by individuals such as Steven Kinney, Aaron "Knobby" Lutz, and Johnny Conrad with their support of youth baseball through the Young American League.

In 1947 professional ball made its comeback when Will Nicholson and Ed Nicholson revived the Bears. They sold the team the following year to the Howsam family. Bob Howsam was the first executive secretary of the Class A Western League, and his family built Bears Stadium, now known as Mile High Stadium, in 1948. In addition to purchasing the Bears, Howsam brought the Denver Broncos to town in 1960 when the American Football League was formed. He also owned the radio station KHOW, which is still on the air; the call letters of the station stand for Howsam.

In 1961, ownership of the Bears transferred to a group head-ed by Gerald Phipps, Ben Stapleton Jr., Cal Kunz, and Edward Hirschfeld. The Bears represented Denver in two Class AAA leagues, the American Association and the Pacific League, until they were sold to John Dikeou and family in 1984 and the team became known as the Denver Zephyrs. The Zephyrs played in Denver through the 1992 season, when they left for New Orleans to make room for the major-league Colorado Rockies.

Obtaining a major-league franchise for Denver was the cul-mination of many years of hard work. From 1901 to 1961, there were only 16 teams in the major leagues. Although some of the teams changed locations, the number of major-league teams remained constant. In 1959, responding to pressure from around the country, the two major leagues made plans to expand. When this expansion failed to bring a team to Denver, Bob Howsam, Ed Johnson (the former governor and senator from Colorado), Branch Rickey of Pittsburgh, and William Shea of New York made plans to form a third major league, the Continental League, with eight new teams. To counter this move, the National and American leagues each expanded their membership by two teams. Even though Denver was again left out of the expansion,

1858-1870	National Association of Base Ball Players. Maintained amateur aspects of the game and standardized rules and equipment.
1871-1875	National Association of Professional Baseball Players. Beginning of professional baseball in America, with teams of salaried players. Players held the balance of power.
1876	National League of Professional Base Ball Clubs. Forerunner to today's National League. Balance of power switched to management.
1884-1946	International League. One of the segregated leagues that existed in America. When Jackie Robinson signed with the Brooklyn Dodgers in 1946 and broke the color barrier, these leagues slowly began to disappear.
1882-1892	American Association, also known as the Beer and Whiskey league because many owners also ran breweries or distilleries. Challenged the National League's monopoly with less regulation, liquor sales, and Sunday games.
1884	Union Association. Formed in opposition to the National League's reserve clause, which bound players to one team. Led to formation of the Western League in 1885.
1885-1890	Brotherhood of Professional Baseball Players. Formed to ease management's control over salaries and disciplinary rules.
1890	Players National League of Base Ball Clubs. Started by players because owners refused to recognize the Brotherhood of Professional Baseball Players as a bargaining agent.
1900	American League formed as a rival to the National League.
1903	Modern two-league structure formalized by The National Agreement.
1914-1915	Federal League. Challenged dominance of the National League and the American League. Its lawsuit against major-league baseball as a monopoly led to a U.S. Supreme Court decision in 1922 that baseball was a sport and thus not subject to the laws of interstate commerce. The major effect of the Federal League was to destroy many minor-league teams, because it drew most of its players from the minors.

BACK ROW—Isringhaus, c; Morgan, 3b; Wollpert, p; To[
CENTER ROW—Cohen, mgr; Lassalle, p; McWhorter, c; [
FRONT ROW—Osorio, p; Rivas, p; Vega, p; Palica, p; Rob[

The 1951 Denver Bears, posing for a card wishing Denverites "Season's Greetings" in front of the three-year-old Bears Stadium.

...ars • 1951

...b; Stewart, p; Schultz, p; Boles, of; Frierson, of
...ms, p; Bruton, of; Lewis, 1b; Jaderlund, of; Behm, trainer
...2b; Gregory, ss; Ries, 3b

— Denver Public Library, Western History Department

◆ WELL KNOWN DENVER BEARS PLAYERS ◆

George Alusik	Ralph Houk	Tim Raines
John Blanchard	Darrell Johnson	Whitey Ries
Steve Boros	Tony Kubek	Bobby Richardson
Billy Bruton	Barry Larkin	Curt Roberts
Andre Dawson	Don Larsen	Chris Sabo
Dizzy Dean	Dutch Leonard	Barney Schultz
Kal Daniels	Lloyd McClendon	Norm Siebern
Eric Davis	Jim McDaniel	Ralph Terry
Rob Dibble	Paul O'Neill	Marv Throneberry
Al Gsorio	Bo Osborne	Joe Tinker
Woodie Held	Bill Pinckard	Coot Veal
Whitey Herzog	Bobby Prescott	Tim Wallach

the major leagues had managed to cut off support for the Continental League.

In the 1970s, businessmen and politicians, such as Denver Mayor Bill McNichols and Governor Richard Lamm, met with baseball owners several times to try to secure a franchise for Denver. For a time, Denver fans' hopes rested with oilman Marvin Davis. In the mid-1970s he tried to purchase the Chicago White Sox and then the Baltimore Orioles and the Oakland A's. Once more, in 1985, Davis tried to bring major-league baseball to Denver with offers to purchase the Oakland A's and San Francisco Giants. All of his offers were rejected.

The pressure increased on the two major leagues as more cities sought baseball. "No more Mr. Nice Guy," cried Colorado Senator Tim Wirth in 1988, stating that he had formed a task force of United States senators from 16 states that were seeking baseball franchises. This committee threatened to introduce legislation to revoke major-league baseball's antitrust-law exemption unless owners provided a timetable for creating expansion teams. Denver's hopes were rekindled on June 14, 1990, when the National League announced that two new franchises would be awarded in September 1991 and that these two teams would begin to play in 1993.

Denver rushed to make plans to capture this prize. A potential ownership group was announced on August 14, 1990. (It would later change as some members dropped out and new ones were added.) Denver-area voters passed a 0.1% sales tax to build a baseball-only stadium, one of the requirements of the National League. When league representatives visited the city in March 1991, the welcome mat was out — banners flew, bells rang, and crowds gathered. Governors from four surrounding states came to champion Denver's cause.

On June 10, 1991, the official announcement came down from the National League that the two expansion teams would be Miami and Denver. The city's dream had come true, and work soon began on a new stadium that would revitalize a historic north downtown neighborhood.

BALLPARKS
OLD AND NEW

"The ballpark is as much a personality as the players on the field…The ballpark also serves as a shrine to America's pastoral roots."

— Colorado Rockies
The Inaugural Season

The large crowds watching the Colorado Rockies' first season set records, but going out to the ball game is nothing new in Denver. For more than a century, Denver residents have been frequenting baseball grounds, from undeveloped open fields to the grandiose new Coors Field. Bert Davis, who managed and played for Denver Athletic Club teams in the nineteenth century, reminisced in the Rocky Mountain News about spectators who would watch as many as three or four games on a Sunday afternoon. "The old Three Mile House on Riverside Cemetery Road was a hot spot for ball fans," he recalled. "They used to hitch the old gray mare to the Sunday buggy and watch teams play ball — and claim they had an entertaining day."

One of the city's first formal fields for baseball was the Broadway Grounds, located at Broadway, Lincoln, Colfax, and Sixteenth streets, about where the Regional Transportation District's Civic Center Station stands today. The grounds were occasionally used for baseball, with grandstands erected for big games and other special events. Years later, this was the setting for the Festival of Mountain and Plain, organized by the merchants of Denver to stimulate the economy after the Silver Crash of 1893 and to celebrate the successful harvest of 1895. The festival was held periodically between the years of 1895 and 1912 and was reborn in 1983 as A Taste of Colorado: The Festival of Mountain and Plain.

Another early Denver field was located between Thirty-second and Thirty-third and Larimer and Market streets. In 1885, shareholders raised $900 to cover the cost of improvements to the site. Sod was installed, stands were built, awnings were erected to shelter the spectators, and light refreshments were made available. This was the site in 1885 where Denver's first all-salaried team successfully played its first season and also the home field of the 1886 Western League pennant winning team. According to baseball historian Jay Sanford, tickets were twenty-five cents for adults and ten cents for children, and post-season

Broadway Grounds, located near the site of the Regional Transportation District
Civic Center Station, across Lincoln and Colfax from where the state Capitol is

now located. This site was used for baseball beginning in 1862. The building in the background is the old Arapahoe County Courthouse. — *Jay Sanford collection*

games drew from 1,000 to 4,000 spectators. In October 1886, the Rocky Mountain News opined, "The largest assemblage the state has at any time contained assembled yesterday to see Denver Nine play the final game in the series with St. Joe and win the championship of the West — Denver will fly the pennant next year."

As the demand for baseball fields grew, River Front Park, a privately owned recreational area developed by John Brisbane Walker, provided another baseball diamond for use. It was located between Sixteenth and Nineteenth streets and the Platte River and Bassett Street. River Front encompassed more than 50 acres, and the baseball grounds were located in the center of a half-mile race track; professional baseball was played here during the 1887 and 1888 seasons.

According to an article published in March 1887 at the time of its construction, the River Front grounds "will be considerably larger than the present grounds [at Larimer and Thirty-second

Rendering of the 1885 Larimer Street Base Ball Park. This area, near Coors Field, was selected by Westword in 1994 as the "Best New Old Neighborhood" in metro Denver. The illustration is by Karle Seydel, revitalization director of the Ballpark Neighborhood. Westword named Seydel the Denver area's "Best Neighborhood Booster" in 1993. — *Copyright Karle Seydel, Denver Ballpark Cards.*

streets]. Overlooking the race track and ball grounds a commodious grandstand will be erected. In front will be a row of private boxes, each one capable of holding a dozen persons. Extending back of the boxes will be built tiers of seats. Back of these a promenade will extend. The grandstand will be gaily decorated. Twenty flagpoles will rise above it, from where gaily colored bunting will fly." River Front's entire grounds were lighted by electricity and enhanced by shade trees planted throughout the park.

Walker was a man of varied interests. He developed Berkeley Park and donated 50 acres of it to Regis College; he owned *Cosmopolitan* magazine, which he later sold to William Randolph Hearst; and he introduced outdoor singing in the Red Rocks area.

In 1889, professional baseball moved to a new park built at Broadway and Cherry Creek. This park, known as the Athletic Park or Base Ball Park, was developed by the Denver Tramway Company to increase its ridership. The Tramway Company leased two blocks of land for 24 years and spent $11,000 to build grandstands, bleachers, lockers, and an adequate playing surface. The first game at the new park was played March 31, 1889, between an Aspen team and the Denvers; it was not well-attended because of wet weather. Both professional baseball, when Denver fielded a Western League team, and semi-pro ball, when it didn't, was played here between 1889 and the turn of the century. In 1899, however, a fire heavily damaged this site.

In 1900, George Tebeau rebuilt the Base Ball Park to give his new Western League team a place to play. Tebeau reconstructed the field, drainage system, grandstands, bleachers, and other seating at a cost of almost $5,000. The Western League Baseball Park had a grandstand that was 100 feet long and accommodated 2,000 people with private boxes on the upper level. Additional seating in the bleachers held 1,500 people. These improvements and the city's first parade for a baseball team got the 1900 baseball season off to a good start, as the Rocky Mountain News enthusiastically reported: "The opening of the baseball season

was intensely gratifying to the fans of the city and forebodes much for the success of league ball in this city. During the parade, which was entirely new and novel for Denver, the players of both teams were made to feel that they would be appreciated. It may be inferred that Tebeau and his men will make a strong bid to make the pennant fly at Broadway." The Denver Nine did do well enough that year to capture the pennant.

On the evening of July 16, 1901, there was another fire at the site. This fire was of questionable origins. "Harry M. Rhoads and his sister saw a man jump over the fence on the Broadway side, enter a buggy, and drive out Broadway just as the fire started," the Denver Times reported. "The stands, the fence, and buildings, except a few rows of seats, were entirely consumed by fire last night at 10:55 o'clock. The damage is estimated at $5,000 on which $4,000 is placed through the agencies of D.C. Packard [president of Denver's Western League team] and Bartels Bros."

This fire was a blow to the Denvers, as The Denver Post lamented on July 17: "The team has just returned from a most disastrous trip abroad and expected to make up a great deal of ground lost in the pennant race on its home ground." But work was started quickly to rebuild the park. On July 18 the Rocky Mountain News reported that "100 men will begin work this morning on a larger scale big grandstand at Broadway Park....The management yesterday awarded a contract to Stocker and Frazer, builders of the grandstands for the Festival of Mountain and Plain. The entire contract will be completed by next week. The

The Athletic Park, or Base Ball Park, located where Broadway crosses Cherry Creek. This park was constructed in 1900 after the old stands on the site were destroyed by fire in 1899. — *Jay Sanford collection*

seating capacity at the new structure will be 50 percent more than heretofore."

The Denver team eventually recovered from the disruption and baseball returned to the Athletic/Base Ball Park. The rebuilt grounds continued to be used until 1922 for baseball. In 1922, Denver businessmen put up the money to acquire a minor-league team from Joplin, Missouri, but the owners could not come to terms with Tebeau to use the park at Broadway and Cherry Creek. Instead, they hastily constructed a new ballpark at Exposition and Broadway, catty-corner to the 1882 Exposition Baseball Grounds. The new park was known as Merchants Park because the site was leased from the Merchants Biscuit Company, now part of Keebler Company.

Merchants Park, seating 8,000 people, was built at a cost of $20,000. According to a Rocky Mountain News article, "thousands of feet of lumber will be used in the stands and it will all be purchased in Denver." Builders had to complete the ballpark in just five weeks to be ready for the season's first game. They almost made it. On April 28, 1922, the Denver Bears played the Wichita Witches, who won 4 to 1. After opening day, newspapers reported that, "One-half of the stands were not painted yet. There was a new coat of yellow paint wasted on the dugout but it made a beautiful mess of sweaters, gloves and other paraphernalia."

The new owners were keen promoters of the team. On opening day, the team was greeted by a "Monster Parade," in which a new bear mascot named "Babe Ruth" rode in a limousine. There was a standing offer of four pounds of butter for the Bear player who "first creeps, sneaks, slips, or slides into home plate," and a ten-pound box of candy from Brecht Candy to players who hit the company's sign on the right-field fence. Newspapers ran "Do You Know Your Denver Team?" contests in which free tickets were awarded to people who could correctly identify pictures of the players. All of these things led to a successful season opener, as the Rocky Mountain News reported: "10,000 Throng Park at Opening of Base Ball Season."

Milton Anfenger purchased Merchants Park in 1923, and his brother Fred ran it until 1946. With its 457-foot center-field fence, the park was not a home-run hitter's paradise. Only three home runs were known to have been hit over center field in the park's 26-year history. One was hit by Babe Ruth on a barnstorming tour in 1927, another by Josh Gibson, playing in a Denver Post Tournament, and the third by another Denver Post Tournament player by the name of Judy Cline.

Colorado Sports Hall of Famer Frank Haraway, a sportswriter and official scorekeeper for the Bears for decades and for the Rockies when they began to play, remembers that the outfield was almost all rocks and that in Merchants Park a no-hitter or a 1-0 game was almost unimaginable due to the poor field conditions. "Frequently, what looked to be a harmless infield single could hit a rough or hard spot and take an erratic bounce all the way to the fence for a triple," Haraway recalled. There was a knothole in the fence where kids could watch the game from the outside, and Haraway remembers a hole in the wire screen by his box seat through which the players would poke their bats for a good-luck rub.

The press box, box seats, and bleachers were in no better shape than the field. Over the years the park was called the

Spectators at the Base Ball Park, photographed in 1910. Note the incline of the field, which allowed for bicycle racing at the park. — *Jay Sanford collection*

"Termite Capital of the World," "That Ramshackle Merchants Park," a "Monumental Pile of Splinters," and the "Worst Ball Park in America."

Lights were added to the stadium in 1931, four years before Crosley Field in Cincinnati became the first major-league field to have lights. But, as with the field and the grandstands, the lights proved to be inadequate. In their book Denver, Bill Barker and Jackie Lewen wrote, "At one dimly lit night game, a realistic out-fielder showed up wearing a miner's lamp on his cap."

The Merchants Park grandstands were condemned in 1945 after a grand jury found the park unsafe for spectators three days before the semi-pro Victory League season was to open. That year, baseball was played on other fields throughout the city while renovations and improvements to Merchants Park were made; the park reopened the following year. Anfenger sold the troubled field in 1946 to J.F. McNaul and Arthur Cowperthwaite, a member of the family that at various times owned much of the Coors Field site and operated lumber yards there. But despite the new owner-ship, Merchants Park's days were numbered.

According to long-time Bears owner Bob Howsam, minor-league baseball returned to Denver after World War II when Jack Carberry and Dave Garland, Sr. organized a five-team Western League. To find a much-needed sixth team, they sought help from Senator Ed Johnson, because they knew of his interest in baseball and he obtained a commitment from Lincoln, Nebraska, to field a team. Howsam said adequate playing fields were a big concern of the new league. Omaha had no field and played at Council Bluffs; Lincoln had an alfalfa field on which a wooden stadium was constructed in just 30 days; Des Moines put up snow fences to mark the outfield perimeter in a city park; and Sioux City nailed the final touches to its center-field fence right before the first game. Pueblo had an older but well-maintained stadium. The new Bears team, owned by Charley Boettcher, Ed Nicholson, and Will Nicholson, played at the reopened Merchants Park in 1947. After a disappointing year of attendance, exacerbated by the stadium's poor condition, the team was sold to the Howsam family. They operated the team under the name Rocky Mountain Empire Sports Inc.

In order to make the franchise a financial success, the Howsams decided a new stadium was essential and began scouting sites. Three locations were considered: the old Flying Field School at Interstate 70 and Colorado Boulevard; the site of the Cherry Creek Shopping Center, an open field at the time; and a

Newly built Merchants Park in 1922. This was the home field of the Denver Bears and for Denver Post Tournaments. — *Jay Sanford collection*

location between Seventeenth and Twentieth streets and Federal Boulevard and Bryant Street, then a city dump. Dave Garland, Sr., president of the Victory League, had been eyeing the latter site since 1936 as he drove by the dump on the way to his son's baseball practice. Garland suggested this location to Senator Ed Johnson as a home for the Bears, and Mayor Benjamin Stapleton said he would sell the land for one dollar to anyone who would build a ballpark on it. However, this opportunity was lost when Stapleton was defeated by Quigg Newton; the newly elected mayor offered the property instead for its appraised value of $33,000.

Construction soon began at the Federal Boulevard site, but until the new Bears Stadium could be completed, the team had to play home games at Merchants Park for a few more months. At 10:52 P.M. on July 26, 1948, the end of an era came at Merchants Park when the Bears beat the Sioux City Sioux by the score of 8-5. Merchants Park's passing was not mourned. As authors Barker and Lewen wrote, "This somewhat archaic ball pasture is now gone and nobody cares." Sportswriter Carberry stated: "The passing of Merchants Park leaves us with nothing but a feeling of joy and happiness and thanksgiving." For all its faults, Merchants Park was home to some of the best baseball and baseball players that Denver has ever seen. When baseball wasn't

A 1947 photo of Merchants Park after it was remodeled but still without much grass in the outfield. Baseball Hall of Famers Babe Ruth, Cool Papa Bell, Rogers Hornsby, Buck Leonard, Johnny Mize, Satchel Paige, Lou Gehrig, Josh Gibson, Grover Cleveland Alexander, Oscar Charleston, and Bob Feller all played here. — *Jay Sanford collection*

played there, the park hosted boxing and wrestling matches, football games, motorcycle and midget auto races, and even a bullfight.

Bears Stadium was built at a cost of $250,000 and was the first concrete, amphitheater-style stadium in Denver. It was an immediate improvement over Merchants Park. As a fan reminisced in the Rocky Mountain News on the fortieth anniversary of Bears Stadium, by then known as Mile High Stadium, "The fans went from the wooden benches of the old park to theater-style seats at Bears Stadium. The players went from playing on a dirt and gravel infield to the new grass just planted at Bears." The first game played in Bears Stadium was on August 14, 1948, when once again the Bears played the Sioux City Sioux. All 6,200 reserved and box seats and more than 4,000 general-admission tickets were purchased to watch Ken Polivka pitch a game against Nick Andromidas of the Sioux — the same pitchers who closed down Merchants Park. Once again the Bears were victorious, this time by a score of 9-5.

Box seats at the new park cost $1.25 each, reserved seats $1.10, and general admission ninety cents. One could buy a cherry Coke for a nickel. The papers reported, "Denver baseball fans, an estimated 11,000 of them, thronged the new ballpark to make its official opening a success....Each player on opening day received a hand-carved wooden grizzly bear as a memento of this occasion."

Bears Stadium was put together in an unusual way. Because of restrictions imposed by World War II, nails could not be used and the contractors were forced to build with bolts. Bob Howsam found this to be amusing because bolts use much more metal than nails. Construction was not completed by opening day. There were only cement seats from first to third base, and the rest of the seating area was a dirt hill. Work continued, however, and within a few years there was seating for 18,523 fans, with folding chairs in the boxes and individual wooden seats between the boxes and the bleachers.

Photo of Bears Stadium in 1948 showing its amphitheater design. — *Jay Sanford collection*

The new park appeared to be a financial success. In 1948, the total attendance of 205,000 was double the number of spectators at Merchants Park the year before. Attendance the next year totaled 463,029, which outdrew two major-league teams, the St. Louis Browns and the Philadelphia Phillies. Attendance varied with the interest in baseball, from as low as 161,120 in 1959 to a peak of 565,000 in 1980.

As early as the late 1950s, Denver's baseball stadium became a factor in attempts to lure major-league teams to the city. The major leagues' bluebook, a manual for club owners, required that their stadiums have seating for 35,000. Combined with plans to obtain an American Football League franchise, this led the Howsam family to build the south stands in 1960, expanding seating capacity to 26,623. Portable seating in the east field increased the seating to about 35,000.

In June 1961, ownership of the Bears and Broncos, as well as the stadium, transferred to a group headed by Gerald Phipps, Ben Stapleton, Jr., Cal Kunz, and Edward Hirschfeld. Six years later, a public fund drive raised $1.8 million to enable the city of Denver to purchase Bears Stadium. The city then renamed the field Mile High Stadium. In a 1968 expansion, made possible with the passage of a $3-million bond issue, all five tiers of the west stands were built. A ten percent surcharge on tickets allowed a five-tier addition to the north stands in 1975, bringing the total seating capacity to 54,100, and the completion of the 21,031-seat east stands in 1976, increasing seating to 75,131. The construction of luxury sky boxes in 1988 was the last expansion, adding 1,000 seats.

Mile High Stadium was used for both football and baseball. When the 90-million-pound east stands were constructed, they were designed to move forward 145 feet for football or back for baseball. The stands sit on 165 water bearings designed like huge inner tubes. To move the stands, water is pumped from a 60,000-gallon holding tank into these tubes, raising the stands one and a half inches off the concrete slab. Oil-hydraulic cranes at each end of the stand then move it in six-foot intervals. The move that takes two hours and five minutes is monitored by television that shows the stands lined up against a giant yardstick to keep both ends of the stadium moving in sync to avoid cracking the structure. With the east stands moved back for baseball, Mile High Stadium had an unusually large outfield, especially in right center field, and visiting teams had to adjust their tactics to cover such a vast area.

With all of the additions and improvements, Mile High Stadium still was not home to a major-league team. But when Denver was granted a major-league franchise, the Colorado Rockies had to play at Mile High until a new stadium could be built. The Rockies played there during their inaugural season in 1993 and for part of the 1994 season, which came to a premature halt and eventually was canceled after the major-league players went on strike on August 12, 1994.

The last Rockies game at Mile High was played on August 11, 1994, when the home team lost to the Atlanta Braves by a score of 13-0. Greg Maddux, a three-time Cy Young Award winner, was the winning pitcher, and Lance Painter pitched for the Rockies. This game brought to a close Mile High Stadium's 46-year reign as home to Denver's minor- and major-league baseball teams. At a fan-appreciation night held by the Colorado Rockies on September 30, 1994, the home plate from Mile High Stadium was placed on a helicopter by Bob Howsam and Joseph Coors and carried off to be stored until it could be resurrected at Coors Field, the Rockies' new home field.

On June 2, 1989, in anticipation of National League expansion, the Colorado General Assembly passed legislation designed to help lure major-league baseball to the Mile High City. House Bill 1341 allowed for the creation of a stadium district board, the construction of a new stadium, and the laying of a new sales tax, based on the assumptions that Denver would be awarded a major-league franchise and that the sales tax proposal would be approved by voters in the six-county metropolitan area. The bill also created the Colorado Baseball Commission to oversee Denver's efforts to win a franchise. The sales tax election and, eventually, the stadium would be supervised by the seven-member Denver Metropolitan Major League Stadium Board, appointed by Governor Roy Romer.

With the announcement in June 1990 that the National League was expanding by two teams, it became clear that Denver's bid for one of these franchises would have to include a baseball-only stadium. A 0.1 percent sales tax to build the stadium was approved in August and levied on purchases in Adams, Arapahoe, Denver, Douglas, Boulder, and Jefferson counties.

The stadium district board was assisted early in its life by the Colorado Housing and Finance Authority, which acted as an interim administrative body and helped the stadium board with the selection of bond lawyers and investment bankers, the bond sale itself, and the choice of a stadium design, architect, and field site. This responsibility ended after about fifteen months with

◆ THE BALLOT QUESTION ◆

August 14, 1990, Primary Election

Shall, in support of efforts to gain a major league baseball team for Colorado, the Denver Metropolitan Major League Baseball Stadium be authorized to levy and collect a uniform sales tax throughout the district at a rate not to exceed one-tenth of one percent for a period not to exceed twenty years, with the proceeds to be used, along with funds from other sources including the private sector, for the costs relating to a major league baseball stadium to be located within the district, provided that the tax will be levied and collected only upon the granting of a major league franchise by major league baseball to be located within the district?

the appointment of John Lehigh as executive director of the stadium district.

As the search for an architectural firm began, requests for proposals were sent to all local and national firms that had experience in stadium design or that had expressed an interest in the project. The firms that submitted proposals were interviewed by the stadium board, and the firm Hellmuth, Obata and Kassabaum, Inc. (HOK) from Kansas City, Missouri, was selected. This firm had a record of building sports facilities around the world, including Oriole Park at Camden Yards in Baltimore, Joe Robbie Stadium in Miami, Cleveland Stadium, and Comiskey Park in Chicago.

The stadium-site selection began with information packets being sent to all elected officials, planning commissions, and other interested parties in the six-county area. In accordance with House Bill 1341, the Urban Land Institute evaluated the three final proposed sites for the new field: the Sports Complex where Mile High Stadium and McNichols Sports Arena are located; the

The first game played by the Colorado Rockies in Mile High Stadium,
April 9, 1993. This historic event was viewed by 80,227 fans.

— *Gaylon Wampler/Rich Clarkson & Associates*

Gateway area in Auraria, close to where the new Elitch's is located; and downtown Denver at Twentieth and Blake streets. On March 13, 1991, the Twentieth and Blake site was selected because of its relatively low land-acquisition costs, location within walking distance of downtown, good traffic access, and rich history.

Just how far back that history extends was discovered during construction for Coors Field. This entire region was once the floor of a prehistoric ocean, and 20 million years after that a subtropical forest. During excavation, workers discovered a 66-million-year-old dinosaur rib near home plate and plant fossils throughout the grounds. Located close to the Platte River, the site was also a camping ground for nomadic Plains Indians in the late 1700s and first half of the 1800s. When the Denver Pacific Railroad became the link between Denver and the transcontinental railroad through Cheyenne, Wyoming, in 1870, the Coors Field site was its home. The charred timbers from the Denver Pacific Station and its concrete foundation were found by construction crews near the area between first and second bases.

The stadium design that HOK submitted was a traditional urban ballpark with a grass field and close-in seating. The field is

Members of the Ute Indian Nations blessing the Coors Field site, which was once Ute camping grounds. — *Emmett Jordan/Rich Clarkson & Associates*

visible from concession areas and other facilities are close to the seats so fans won't miss much action. J. Bradley Schrock, project designer, said HOK wanted to create a stadium that fits into the historic aspect of the neighborhood but that was obviously built in 1995. The emphasis from the beginning was to involve community and citizen groups both on advisory boards and through public meetings, and to have the project act as a catalyst for redevelopment of the stadium area. Advisory groups included ones on design, transportation, accessibility, media, art, and neighborhood.

Neighborhood characteristics are reflected in the stadium building materials. All of the red bricks in the structure were manufactured by the century-old Robinson Brick and Tile of Denver and mirror the red and cream tones of those found in surrounding buildings. (The three tones of red brick found in the stadium were achieved by firing the bricks for varying lengths of time.) The historic nature of the neighborhood is also visible in the rusticated stone, the buff brick-belt around the stadium, and in the specialized brick work patterned after that of the Ice House and other nearby buildings. As Lehigh said, "If all the red brick and masonry blocks [in the stadium] were laid end to end, they would stretch from Cheyenne, Wyoming, to Pueblo, Colorado."

The exposed structural steel used throughout the stadium reflects the site's railroad heritage and the numerous historic viaducts that were in the area. Details of neighborhood landmarks are incorporated into the design of the stadium, including the canopy at the entrance to Union Station, the colonial pillared entrance of the Union Pacific Freight House, the Daniels & Fisher Tower and Union Station clocks, and the Victorian-like lighting found in Larimer Square and the Lower Downtown Historic District. Three historic buildings are preserved on the Coors Field property: The Union Pacific Freight House at Nineteenth and Wynkoop streets, the Banker's Warehouse Building, and Transport Service Station, both near Twenty-second and Blake streets.

Caissons:	1,387, ranging in depth from 15 to 50 feet
Steel:	8,975 tons
Structural Concrete:	57,000 cubic yards
Masonry:	
Bricks:	1,400,000, extending 177 miles if laid end to end
Cinderblocks:	700,000
Cut stone:	250 tons (from the quarry in Lyons, Colorado)
Paving:	
Concrete:	558,300 square feet
Asphalt:	170,170 square yards
Handrails:	10 miles
Field Lights:	650
Elevators:	11 passenger, 2 freight
Escalators:	9

HOK situated Coors Field so the ballpark is the terminus for all the main streets leading to it, just as Union Station is the terminus for Seventeenth Street. At the end of each of these streets there is a pedestrian tower where people can climb from the street level to their seats. The towers are enhanced by etched glass, terra-cotta columbine blossoms (the Colorado state flower) designed by Denver artist Barry Rose, and step-out bricks that are layered to pick up shadows from the dramatic Colorado sunlight. Reminiscent of the nineteenth century River Front Park, ceremonial flags fly from flagpoles around the exterior.

Opposite: Steel construction of Coors Field, reflecting the design of the old viaducts and railroads of the neighborhood. — *Nate Cox/Rich Clarkson & Associates*

The intent of all involved in the construction was to make Coors Field a year-round, mixed-use facility, and it includes a brew pub, museum, restaurant, store, and headquarters for the Rockies and stadium district personnel. There is also a picnic area and a playground for children.

Works of art were incorporated into the stadium design, funded by the sale of 8,500 personalized brick "pavers" installed on the Wynkoop pedestrian walkway. Three artworks were chosen from 150 designs submitted. A wall sculpture entitled "The Bottom of the Ninth" is located on the exterior of the Banker's Warehouse Building; "The Evolution of the Ball" is a free-standing arch on the Wynkoop Street pedestrian mall; and the mural "The West, The Worker, and The Ball Field" adorns the 100-foot-wide center-field concourse. There is also private and corporate artwork throughout the stadium.

Home plate in Coors Field was located with six global positioning satellites 11,000 miles in space. As a Rocky Mountain News article put it, "By sending a stream of beams down to radio receivers on 'known points' along Blake Street, the satellites framed home plate as a skilled catcher would." Almost everything else in the stadium was measured off the home-plate location: outfield fences, seats, utility cables, and even sewer lines. Lehigh said Coors Field is "a 1.2-million-square-foot facility wrapped around the diamond." The distance from home plate to the left-field fence is 347 feet; center field is a lengthy 420 feet; and right field is 358 feet.

Coors Field has a traditional bluegrass and ryegrass surface with state-of-the-art systems to maintain it. Underneath the playing field is an automated irrigation system with thousands of feet of pipe and wire. The system includes underground heating and sensors that shut off the water automatically when it rains. Coors Field also has an on-site sod farm, with 6,000 square feet

Opposite: Siting of home plate in Coors Field, using a satellite process known as the global positioning system. — *Emmett Jordan/Rich Clarkson & Associates*

"The West, the Worker, and the Ball Field," a hundred-foot-long, eight-foot-high mural by artists Matt O'Neill and Jeff Starr. The piece depicts the history of the Coors Field site, from the days of buffalo to baseball. This section represents a game at Coors Field. An original work owned and commissioned by the Denver Metropolitan Major League Baseball Stadium District.
— *Photo by Jeff Starr*

"The Evolution of the Ball" by Lonnie Hanzon. This colorful archway made of steel, concrete, ceramic, glass mosaic, and wood brings to mind the historic "Welcome" arch outside Union Station. An original work owned and commissioned by the Denver Metropolitan Major League Baseball Stadium District. — *Photo by Lonnie Hanzon*

"The Bottom of the Ninth" by Erick Johnson, one of three pieces of public art incorporated into the stadium. An original work owned and commissioned by the Denver Metropolitan Major League Baseball Stadium District. — *Nate Cox/Rich Clarkson & Associates*

Rusticated stone and blue and white terra-cotta columbine, decorating Coors Field's facade. Use of these materials helps the structure blend in with the historic buildings in the stadium area. — *Nate Cox/Rich Clarkson & Associates*

of sod for field repairs growing behind the warning track in center field. The sod is right in front of the "batter's eye," the green-painted section of fence that gives hitters a clear backdrop for the incoming pitch.

There are 50,249 seats on three levels in the new stadium, with seating for handicapped fans and their companions at every level. Seats located beyond first and third base are angled for sidelong viewing of home plate. Between the first and third level are the club level with indoor and outdoor seating, the members-only Stadium Club dining room, and the press facilities. The press boxes closest to the second level are for the sportswriters, and those closer to the third level are for broadcasters. The seats colored Rockies purple mark the row that is exactly one mile high; all the other seats are Colorado spruce green.

◆ COORS FIELD FACTS — SEATING ◆

Total Seating:	50,249
Field Level Seating:	18,295
Upper Deck Seating:	17,772
Outfield Seating:	Total of 7,805
Left Field:	3,024 benches with backs
Center Field:	2,283 benches without backs ("The Rockpile")
Right Field Mezzanine:	2,598 seats
Club Seating:	4,439
Mezzanine Seating:	2,600
Suites:	52 suites, 735 seats, one suite is a double suite, 4 party suites, 145 seats
Disabled Seating:	449 spaces for wheelchairs, 522 companion seats, and 132 seats without armrests

Concessions:

Service Level:	Main commissary
Main Concourse:	11 concession stands 2 vending areas 2 novelty sales areas 1 deli 1 family concession area
Lower Press Level:	Kitchen and lounge
Club Level:	4 concession stands 2 bars 2 waitress stations 1 pantry 1 central kitchen 1 sweet shop
Suite Level:	6 pantries
Upper Concourse Level:	13 concession stands 2 vending areas 3 novelty sales areas
Restrooms:	35 Women's Restrooms 31 Men's Restrooms 8 family facilities
Parking:	5,200 on-site spaces

The fifty-two luxury suites just below the upper deck rented in 1995 for $70,000 to $100,000 a year. The suites have two rows of outside seats and an enclosed area furnished with tables, chairs, and two television sets. There are also four party suites available to rent for individual games.

In keeping with the old and new design themes, the stadium has two scoreboards. In right field is a manually operated scoreboard that shows scores from other major-league games. The $2.5-million Sony video board, about 23 feet tall and 31 feet

Coors Field under construction, with Denver's skyline in the background, as viewed from Twenty-second Street. — *Nate Cox/Rich Clarkson & Associates*

wide, hangs in left center field. It has 166,464 light elements and is run by controls in the public address and scoreboard room behind home plate. The Daktronics main scoreboard connected to it cost $1.1 million and has 56,320 bulbs, using 400,000 watts of electricity. It measures 74 feet wide by 34 feet high.

Behind the scenes are three clubhouse facilities: one for the umpires, one for the visiting team, and the third for the Rockies. On a tour through the new stadium, Rockies manager Don Baylor told the Rocky Mountain News that the umpires' rooms are "...an apartment. They could live there; that's how big it is." The umpires and the visiting team have their own lockers and shower area. In the 8,600-square-foot visitors' clubhouse, there is a practice batting cage and a pitching area that has the same field dimensions and dirt composition as the outdoor mound and plate.

In addition to all of the amenities provided for the visitors, the 21,700-square-foot Rockies clubhouse has a wave pool, several whirlpool facilities, weight room, an X-ray room, and two pitching and batting areas. "Players who live here full-time can go and work out in the off-season," Baylor said. "No excuses for not winning now." The clubhouse has a dining area, laundry room, video room, locker room, manager's office, interview room, equipment room, luggage storage area and an injury ramp that leads directly from the field. There is also a family lounge with a play area for the players' children.

In all, the new ballpark cost over $215 million to build, of which $30 million was paid by the Colorado Rockies and approximately $185 million was raised through the sale of bonds by the stadium district. The Colorado Rockies will pay annual rent of $2 million to $3 million during the team's seventeen-year lease, and the team is responsible for all operating costs and capital repairs. The stadium district estimates the bonds will be repaid through sales-tax collections in less than nine years, even though the ballot issue allowed for a twenty-year sales tax.

In order to complete Coors Field on time, construction followed a demanding schedule. Some crews worked six days a week, and the typical work day started at 6:30 A.M. and continued to 6:30 P.M. At the height of the project, close to 850 individuals were working on the site. Chuck Simmons, contracts manager for Mortenson/Barton Malow, the project's general contractor, said that "Coors Field was a total team effort."

◆ COORS FIELD FACTS — THE SITE ◆

The Site:	65 acres in all, 3 acres for the field itself
Excavation:	181,000 cubic yards moved; 86,000 cubic yards of backfill
The Field:	
Base:	6,000 tons of sand and peat moss; 3,000 tons of gravel
Infield:	Three to five inches of clay and sand
Grass:	350 pounds of grass seed planted; 2.42 million seeds per pound

The parade down Seventeenth Street that opened the Rockies' inaugural season —
a true part of Denver's baseball heritage. — *Gaylon Wampler/Rich Clarkson &
Associates*

Despite the hectic schedule, Coors Field received national recognition for its safety practices. Moe Mahon, safety engineer on the stadium job, worked with the Occupational Safety and Health Administration to formulate new national standards for protecting workers from dangerous falls. Mahon said the stadium district indicated from the beginning of the project that "safety is just as important as production."

Another area where Coors Field contractors left their mark was in women and minority hiring. William Bell, community relations liaison for the Coors Field project, said that, on a percentage basis, Coors Field had the most women and minority participation ever for a construction job in Colorado. Bell set up meetings with women and minority firms and numerous community organizations to discuss the project's needs, show blueprints, and look for opportunities to break large jobs into smaller packages that would allow minority and small firms to enter the bidding process. Coors Field also reached out to community-based organizations to identify individuals to work on the stadium, a very successful program that provided training as well as employment.

Stewart Ervie, a construction administrator for HOK who worked on Baltimore's Camden Yards ballpark before he came to Denver, said that Denver was unique because of the spirit of the city and its excitement about the stadium project even before its completion: "Nothing compares with this in any other city that we have worked."

If a ballpark is indeed as much a personality as the players on the field, then Coors Field is the best example of Denver's personality — past, present, and future.

The Rockies' purple dinosaur mascot, hatched in 1994 and known affectionately as "Dinger." — *Eric Lars Bakke/Rich Clarkson & Associates*

PLACES AROUND
THE BASES
*THE COORS FIELD
HISTORIC
NEIGHBORHOOD*

"We keep losing marvelous

buildings. Now I think

there's a real hope to preserve

part of the past."

— Karle Seydel
Executive director,
North Larimer Business District

The completion of Coors Field in March 1995 not only provided Denver with a first-class baseball facility, but also stimulated a renaissance for a downtown district rich in history.

The Coors Field neighborhood traces its modern history almost to the days of Denver's settlement. In 1858, a small amount of placer gold was discovered in the Platte Valley. Boosterism and the promise of a new life brought an influx of people to settlements at the confluence of the Platte River and Cherry Creek. But the majority of people who came to Denver seeking their fortune either returned to their homes disappointed or followed their dream of wealth into the mountains in search of the mother lode. After the gold rush, Denver served as a supply town with a population in 1860 of just 4,759 people. Ten years later, the population had grown by a mere ten people.

In 1868, when the Union Pacific placed its transcontinental route through Cheyenne, Wyoming, rather than Denver, many thought the decision would lead to Denver's demise. Charles Albi and Kenton Forrest, in their book *Denver's Railroads*, quote Union Pacific Vice President Thomas C. Durant as saying, "Without the railroad, Denver was too dead to bury."

To avoid this death sentence, a group of Denver citizens raised funds for a railroad line to connect the city to the transcontinental railroad in Cheyenne. This new line, which opened in June 1870, became known as the Denver Pacific Railroad, and it not only saved the city but also led to tremendous growth. Denver became a regional financial, transportation, and supply center, and the downtown area next to the railroad yards became the wholesale and transportation hub for the city. At the time of the 1880 census, Denver's population had grown to more than 35,000 people, and by 1890 its population was more than 100,000.

Along with the increase in population came a major construction boom, with hotels, offices, warehouses, shops, and residences multiplying in Denver. Nowhere was the growth more extreme than in the area surrounding the railroad lines and stations. Today this neighborhood is experiencing a rebirth with the opening of Coors Field.

Coors Field straddles two historic neighborhoods. One is the Lower Downtown Historic District, known as LoDo, which is certified for the National Register of Historic Places. LoDo covers the area between Speer Boulevard on the west and Twentieth Street on the east, and between Wynkoop Street on the north and Market Street on the south. The district also includes the block between Fourteenth and Fifteenth streets on Larimer Street, known as Larimer Square. Dana Crawford, developer of Larimer Square, said of this historic area, "LoDo is not Disneyland. It's Denver's heritage. We need to respect this."

The second neighborhood around Coors Field is the area north of the Lower Downtown Historic District, sometimes called NoDo, for North Downtown, or the Ballpark Neighborhood. Crawford believes that NoDo will develop an image of its own as the area's renaissance continues. Indeed, both areas around Coors Field have characteristics and histories of their own, and every street in the neighborhood has its own background and ambiance.

Before beginning the tour of the Coors Field neighborhood, it's necessary to say a word or two about Denver's street patterns. One could go crazy trying to figure out downtown Denver's streets when comparing old maps to new. Many street names have been changed, and the numbering system was totally revised. In Denver's early days, the streets emanating northeast from the Platte River at West Colfax were named with letters of the alphabet, starting with A Street near what would be Tenth Street in Auraria and extending to Z Street, at today's Thirty-fourth Street. As the city grew, more streets became necessary and the lettering system was changed in 1873 to a numbered system.

In addition, the first platting of the city in 1859 ran parallel to the Platte River and to Cherry Creek rather than following the north-south platting done later for the rest of the city. This left downtown Denver at angles to the rest of the city, and to this day one is never quite sure of the direction one is going in downtown. It also left Denver with many interesting triangular plots where one street system meets another.

THE WALKING TOUR — HOW TO USE THIS GUIDE

This section of the book provides a history and tour of the Coors Field neighborhood and its buildings, covering parts of both downtown historic areas. The guide is organized in the form of a flexible walking tour, or, if you wish, a relaxing arm-chair tour. You may follow our suggested path or delve more deeply into the area by going up and down each street, or by driving around the neighborhood. (Please note that you cannot drive along our walking tour as it's described because it goes the wrong way down several one-way streets.) The suggested walking tour should take an hour and a half to two hours to complete.

The history of each major street on the tour is described as you reach it, followed by details on the important structures and building sites along the street. Please refer to the map at the end of the book if you have any questions about the route along the way.

Each stop on the tour is coded in the text and on the map as follows:

● Buildings that are still standing. These buildings are included on the walking tour.

■ Buildings that are no longer standing or have been replaced.

◆ Important buildings or building sites close to this area but not included in the walking tour. We suggest you drive to these buildings to visit them if you are interested.

One manifestation of Denver's history is the many buildings in the Coors Field neighborhood that have National Register or Denver Landmark status. As you follow the walking tour of the Coors Field neighborhood, you will notice many buildings with one or both of the following designations.

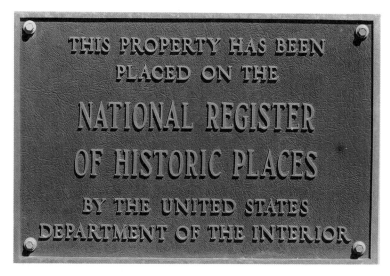

NATIONAL REGISTER DESIGNATION

This plaque indicates a property is on the National Register of Historic Places, the nation's list of properties that are important to communities, regions, and states in their history, architecture, engineering, and culture. Although the register is "national," it is designed to include properties of importance to Americans in their own communities, not just the great national landmarks. The registry is overseen by the National Park Service, and the properties included may be sites, buildings, or whole districts. Properties are nominated by individuals, organizations, state and local governments, and federal agencies. — *Randy Brown Photographer*

DENVER LANDMARK DESIGNATION

This plaque indicates a property is a Denver Landmark, as designated by the Denver Landmark Commission. To qualify for this designation the structure, site, or district must be at least 30 years old and/or have an extraordinary historical, architectural, or geographical relationship with a person, the city, the state, or the nation. Denver Landmark structures generally have plaques since these are included with landmark designation. National Register buildings on this tour might not have designation plaques because there is an extra fee for these. — *Randy Brown Photographer*

DENVER LANDMARK MARKERS

Plaque for the Lower Downtown Historic District designating a Denver Landmark district, not an individual property. — *Randy Brown Photographer*

There is plenty of on-street parking near Coors Field when the Rockies are not playing, or you can take public transportation to Market Street Station and walk to Coors Field, where our tour begins. Find your way to the front of the stadium's main entrance, at the intersection of Twentieth and Blake streets.

The walking tour descriptions may be broken by a square or a diamond symbol. Read them and continue on the tour to the next circle.

BLAKE STREET

This street was named after Charles H. Blake, who, in October 1858 arrived in Auraria with a partner and eight wagonloads of merchandise and set up the first retail business in the settlement. He was one of the original shareholders and founders of the Denver Town Company. During the 1860s, Blake Street was Denver's principal thoroughfare and the "indiscriminate center of trade," home to a vast variety of businesses, including many saloons, gambling houses, boarding houses, blacksmith shops, banks, retail businesses, and corrals. Look to your right toward the 1900–2000 block of Blake Street. This block is an excellent example of late nineteenth-century and early twentieth-century commercial architecture. Most of the buildings have been converted into business and residential lofts, studios, and storefronts.

The 1700, 1800, and 1900 blocks of Blake Street all are certified for the National Register of Historic Places and have Denver Landmark status as part of the Lower Downtown Historic District. The street signs in the LoDo area say "Lower Downtown Denver Historic District" on one side and the word "Mizpah" on the other. "Mizpah" was emblazoned across an arch spanning Seventeenth Street in front of Union Station from 1906 to 1931. In Hebrew, it means, "The Lord watch between me and thee when we are absent one from another." The other side of the Union Station arch said "Welcome" to travelers arriving in Denver.

❶ Coors Field

The right to name Denver's new baseball stadium was sold to the Coors family of Golden by the Colorado Rockies to help obtain the funds necessary to bring a major-league baseball franchise to Denver. The field was named for the Coors Brewing Company and for the family that has operated the brewery and subsidiary businesses in Colorado since 1873. In addition to the naming rights, the Coors family has a major equity interest in the Colorado Rockies. In the words of Peter Coors, chief executive officer of Coors Brewing Company, "The Coors family is interested in baseball in the same way the rest of the community is interested in baseball. Family members have played baseball and have sponsored various aspects of baseball for decades, and we have been pleased that we could have contributed to the successful effort of bringing baseball to Colorado."

Offices of the Colorado Rockies Baseball Club occupy the second and third floors of the stadium at this corner and overlook the neighborhood. The Rockies and Coors Field already have had positive spill-over effects on the area, including new sidewalks, trees, and period lighting.

Coors Field under construction in its urban setting. — *photo by Chuck Simmons*

Businesses are now locating in many historic buildings, further helping to revitalize the neighborhood.

The Colorado Rockies also have placed a priority on youth programs and on outreach to local and regional communities. The team has established two foundations: The Colorado Rockies Baseball Club Foundation and the Rockies Charity Fund, a fund of the Robert R. McCormick Tribune Foundation. The Rockies Foundation was formed in 1991 with an emphasis on underprivileged and at-risk youth. The Charity Fund, begun in 1993, also targets youth programs and contains certain health programs.

In a letter explaining the Rockies Foundation, Jerry McMorris, president, chairman, and chief executive officer of the Rockies, stated, "The Rockies Foundation offers programs that are designed to improve the quality of life for children in the region. The major focus is on youth, youth literacy, youth at risk, and drug and alcohol abuse. The outreach programs were started to return the favor of the genuine, warm support that we (the Rockies) received during our first year in major-league baseball."

Walk along the front of the stadium to the corner of Twenty-first and Blake Streets.

② DIAMOND MINE STORE AND ROCKY MOUNTAIN BASEBALL MUSEUM
Twenty-first and Blake streets

The museum and Colorado Rockies store are open year-round. The museum displays memorabilia from the Colorado Rockies and baseball in the Rocky Mountain region, as well as traveling exhibits. The store sells Colorado Rockies memorabilia and some items from other major-league baseball teams.

Continue down Blake Street to Twenty-second Street.

Street signs hanging from lights in Lower Downtown, reminiscent of the past. One side says "Lower Downtown Denver Historic District," and the other says "Mizaph" — a Hebrew greeting that was written on the old arch across Seventeenth Street in front of Union Station. — *Randy Brown Photographer*

❸ BANKER'S WAREHOUSE COMPANY BUILDING
Twenty-second and Blake streets

Incorporated into the Coors Field structure is the Banker's Warehouse Building, a five-story warehouse built in 1913. One of three historic properties saved on the stadium district land, the building houses the offices of the Denver Metropolitan Major League Baseball Stadium District, the physical plant for the stadium, the kitchen for stadium concessionaire ARAMARK, and the Sandlot Microbrewery and its adjacent restaurant. The ales, stouts, lagers and pilsners, produced here by Coors Brewery Company are available only at the Microbrewery, its adjacent restaurant and at Coors Field concessions.

❹ "THE BOTTOM OF THE NINTH"
Twenty-second and Blake streets

Located on the Twenty-second Street side of the Banker's Warehouse building, this is one of three public works of art that were funded by the sale of personalized brick pavers placed into the Wynkoop Pedestrian Walkway. Designed by artist Erick Johnson, it is a kinetic neon and aluminum-relief depiction of a player sliding into home plate, with the umpire making the call. The call varies, so look up to see if the player is safe or out when the ball is thrown.

❺ TRANSPORT SERVICE STATION
Twenty-second and Blake streets

This is the second historic structure to be included in the Coors Field design. Originally located at 2001 Blake Street, the building was erected in 1934 and is a prime example of an art-deco service station. At one point, the station was painted white; now it has been power-washed back to its original brown and red brick glaze.

6 KAMINSKY BARREL COMPANY BUILDING
Twenty-second and Blake streets

This structure was built in 1928 as storage space for wood and metal barrels. Notice the Kaminsky sign painted on the side of the building. In Denver in the late nineteenth and early twentieth centuries, sign painters were an everyday necessity for many companies. In addition to identifying the location of businesses, they were needed for labeling and pricing retail items. Many of these signs have been covered up by newer signs, but weathering is revealing the older ones. The old signs often were thought to be works of art, and the painters sometimes signed them. As you proceed through the neighborhood, be sure to look for these hidden treasures.

Note: Remember the text may be broken by a square or a diamond symbol. Read the information and continue on the tour to the next circle.

1 McPHEE AND McGINNITY BUILDING
2301 Blake Street
National Register designation

This building was constructed in three stages in 1913, 1919, and 1950. It was originally designed by Fisher and Fisher, one of the oldest architectural firms in Denver. William Fisher began practice in Denver in 1892, and his brother Arthur joined the firm in 1897. This firm designed the Neusteters Building, the Midland Savings Building, the Voorhies Memorial in Civic Center Park, and the Phipps Mansion in Belcaro. Fisher and Fisher also designed the Windsor Farm Dairy Building and the BDT Building, which you will see later on this tour.

The McPhee & McGinnity Building housed two pioneer businesses. The first was the McPhee & McGinnity Company, which was the largest supplier of building materials in the

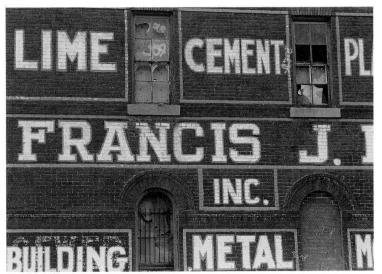

Francis J. Fisher Building. Many buildings in downtown Denver retain the signage of their previous occupants. This in itself is a historic record. — *Randy Brown Photographer*

Rocky Mountain region from the end of the nineteenth century into the 1920s. Also a major contractor, the company helped construct much of the downtown area and supplied the lumber for construction of the Moffat Tunnel in the 1920s. McPhee had 13 children. John Bid McPhee, one of his sons, played major-league baseball with Cincinnati for 18 years, and there is a movement to put him in the Baseball Hall of Fame.

The Denver Fire Clay Company, first listed at this address in 1937, occupied the building for twenty years. This firm was founded in 1882 as a chemical and drug business that created crucibles used for assaying ore from mines. The founder, Joab Otis Bosworth, came to Denver in 1871, worked as a bookkeeper at the Bank of Denver and as a druggist before forming the Denver Fire and Clay Company. He died in a chemical explosion in 1890.

◆2 PACIFIC EXPRESS STABLE
2363 Blake Street
National Register designation

This building was constructed in 1888 and was used as a stable until 1910. Pacific Express transported railroad freight throughout the city at a time when horses, wagons, and buggies were the typical means of transportation. Francis J. Fisher bought the building in 1913. (Note the name Fisher added to the entrance.) The Fisher Company sold building supplies such as lime, cement, plaster, fire brick, and sewer pipe. The company remained at this site until 1974.

Note: Buildings with a square are no longer standing. Continue walking to the next circle symbol for the tour.

■1 KUNER PICKLE COMPANY
Twenty-second and Blake street

John C. Kuner came from St. Louis to found the J. C. Kuner and Son Vinegar Company in 1872. He was bought out by his brother, Max, in 1883. The firm, now known as Kuner-Empson Company, operated its headquarters and processing and packing plant on Blake and Twenty-second Street beginning in 1884. The tomato-canning plant was located on the Coors Field site, between Twenty-first and Twenty-second and Wazee Street, with railroad trackage the entire length of the building. At Twenty-second and Blake, across Blake Street from the stadium, were the headquarters, shipping room, pickle factory, and mustard, apple butter, and bean kitchens. Kuner employees often took their coffee breaks at the St. Louis House, located down the street at 2112–2118 Blake Street. If you purchased a beer there at noon, you'd receive a free meal. Around the turn of the century, employees worked six days a week for their $4 to $10 weekly salary. By 1917,

Kuner's factory and offices had moved to Brighton, Colorado. *Walk back to the corner of Twenty-first and Blake streets.*

2 DENVER PACIFIC DEPOT
Between Twenty-first and Twenty-second and Wazee streets

The last spike ceremony to celebrate the connection of the Denver Pacific Railroad to the transcontinental railway was held here on June 24, 1870. The spike was made of silver mined in Georgetown, Colorado. The first railway station in Denver, the Denver Pacific Depot, was built in 1870, adjacent to this site. It was quickly replaced by the Denver Pacific/Kansas Pacific Depot, an imposing two-story brick structure that was used by railroad companies until 1881. This station's burnt remains were discovered close to the area between first and second base during the excavation of Coors Field.

3 PUROX BUILDING/WINDSOR FARM DAIRY BUILDING
Twenty-first and Blake streets

The Purox Building was erected in 1926 for the Denver Transit & Warehouse Company. Mr. Howard, owner of the company, built Denver's first bonded warehouse for this business at another location in Denver in 1882. The facade of the Purox Building has been saved.

The Windsor Farm Dairy Building, also located on this site, first was a stable for horses pulling the company's dairy wagons, and later a truck garage. This building again housed horses and wagons during World War II when it was impossible to obtain enough gasoline to make deliveries. According to long time dairy employees the horses knew the delivery route so well that they would stop at the correct homes and businesses automatically. In the early 1940's the cost of a carton of cottage cheese was 9¢ and a quart of milk 16¢.

Windsor Farm Dairy was sold in 1928 to Beatrice Foods. The terra-cotta sign from this building has been preserved.

Walk down Twenty-first Street, away from the stadium, to Market Street.

4 HOP ALLEY

By 1870, Denver's Chinese residential and business district was centered on the alley between Blake and Market streets, known locally as "Hop Alley," and spilled over into adjoining blocks. Early Chinese settlers lived between Sixteenth and Seventeenth streets on Wazee Street and were predominantly displaced workers from the California gold camps and the railroads. Most of the residents of Hop Alley were single men, because cultural and economic demands forced their wives and daughters to stay home in China to care for their parents and family. It was a lonely existence in Denver for the early Chinese. Most of them ran hand laundries because this business required little capital investment or training. According to the Colorado Historical Society's Essays and Monographs magazine, there were 238 Chinese in the city of 35,629 in 1880. Of these, 202 were associated with the laundry business. Because of their different mode of dress and customs they had a hard time intermingling with the other settlers. At times, prejudice against the Chinese ran high, and on October 31, 1880, there was an anti-Chinese riot. One man was hung and several residences and businesses were destroyed.

Opium and gambling dens also existed, and tongs, the Chinese secret societies, unofficially kept the rule. The opium and gambling dens stayed open until legislation enacted in 1912 forced them underground within the next few years. Denver's early Chinese population peaked at 980 in 1890, and by 1900 census numbers had decreased to 306. As the Chinese community matured, the Chinese residents of

Hop Alley, the unofficial name for the center of Denver's Chinese neighborhood. This is a 1929 photo. It was not unusual for businesses in the downtown area to have their primary entrances situated in an alley. — *Denver Public Library, Western History Department*

Chinese residents of Denver in 1925. Although the early Chinese community was mainly a "bachelor" society, things had changed by this time, and the community had its own YMCA and schools. — *Colorado Historical Society*

Denver were represented in the professions and many different kinds of businesses.

MARKET STREET

Market Street was first called McGaa Street for William McGaa, who, along with William Larimer, named most of the original streets in the downtown area. McGaa claimed to be the disowned son of an English baron. He left home to go to sea and eventually ended up in the Pikes Peak region, married to Wewatta of the Arapahoe Indian Nation. McGaa was an original shareholder in the townships of Denver and its predecessors, Auraria and St. Charles. He was a dissolute character and caused so many disruptions that the city fathers changed the street name in 1866 from McGaa to Holladay in honor of Ben Holladay, who, with his cousin Bela Hughes, ran the Central Overland, California, and Pikes Peak Express Company Stagecoach Lines. After the railroad brought substantial growth to Denver, Holladay Street was known for open-air meat and produce markets at its Cherry Creek end, and for its red-light district, mainly between Nineteenth and Twenty-second streets. North of Twenty-third Street, Holladay Street was a residential area.

Because of the negative connotations associated with the street, the Holladay family petitioned the city to change its name, and in 1889 Holladay was changed to Market Street. The residential portion of the street was renamed Walnut Street.

7 PIGGLY WIGGLY MACMARR
2101–2125 Market Street

The regional Piggly Wiggly franchise was started in
Colorado Springs as the Piggly Wiggly Grimes Company. It
introduced new concepts in grocery retailing, with automatic
scales for weighing goods and a turnstile entrance and baskets
for customers so they could serve themselves instead of waiting for clerks to find goods. Colorado Sports Hall of Famer
Frank Haraway's father moved the headquarters to Denver in
1918. After a merger with MacMarr, the company constructed this building in 1927 for warehouse and office space. In
1931, Piggly Wiggly's 1,400 stores merged with Safeway; the
name of the store was changed to Safeway in 1936.

3 TIMPTE BROTHERS WAGON COMPANY
2312 Market Street

This structure was built in 1891 for the Timpte
Brothers Wagon Company. Brothers William and August
Timpte had trained as blacksmiths under their father. In
1891 they merged their individual businesses into one and
moved to this location. Listings for William Timpte in the
Denver city directory go back to 1882, when he is listed as a
blacksmith.

The new company was listed in an 1892 directory as
"Blacksmith, horseshoer, carriage and wagon maker." Timpte
Brothers designed and manufactured buggies, carriages, and
light spring wagons for mining, commerce, and local delivery,
in addition to heavy brewery wagons. The brothers' company
became the largest vehicle supplier in the mountain states.

Opposite: The Piggly Wiggly MacMarr Building, in the foreground. Built by the
company for its regional headquarters, this building and the one behind it exhibit
some of the interesting architectural details found on older buildings. — *Randy
Brown Photographer*

This building originally totaled 12,500 square feet, with a wooden floor and a forge. Railroad tracks came right to the building, which made loading and unloading easy. The company remained at this location for fifty years. Some of its last wagons were made for the Tivoli Brewery in the late 1920s. The company then went from manufacturing wagons to building bodies for early truck chassis. Early delivery-truck bodies were built mostly on a Model T chassis, and farm bodies, local delivery vans, and highway transports followed. Some early local companies using Timpte truck bodies were Manitou Springs Water, the Red and White stores, Fred Davis Furniture, and Dr. Pepper Company. This company still exists under the name Timpte Industries Inc. and manufactures bodies for large trucks and grain trailers.

Walk down Market Street toward Twentieth Street. Stop at 2015 Market Street. The 1700, 1800, and 1900 blocks of Market Street all are certified for the National Register and have the Denver Landmark designation as part of the Lower Downtown Historic District.

You are standing at the heart of Denver's early red-light district, which was known as "The Row" or "The Line." At one time there were more than 1,000 "everybody's and nobody's" women working on Market Street, which raged until 1912 when a reform slate was elected in Denver and forced prostitution underground.

Prostitutes worked either in "cribs" or in elegant bordellos — or places that were somewhere in between. A crib was usually a rented one- or two-room area with a window for soliciting customers who were in the street. A "soiled dove" working out of a crib earned twenty-five cents to two dollars per customer, with one dollar being the usual fee, and she could have as many as twenty-five customers a night. At the other end of the scale, a "bride of the multitude" who worked in brothels earned an average of five dollars to thirty dollars per night, with fewer customers and much more elegant surroundings.

Life for women who worked on this street was not enviable. Many were addicted to opium, liquor, or other drugs, and most of their income went for room and board and clothing. The fancy ladies in the "houses" split their take 50–50 with the madams. As one fallen woman said in answer to censure, "If we were to give up lives of sin and shame, there'd be no place for us to go. Nobody would have anything to do with us. Society would spurn us. And so we have to stay here to earn our bread and butter." The women suffered most of the blame for the Market Street trade, but they couldn't do business without customers. On March 16, 1909, evangelist Gypsy Smith said, "You've no right, you men, to spurn a woman in the sunshine and visit her by night."

8 AMERICAN LEGION POST/CATHAY POST/NISEI #185
2015 Market Street

In the 1940s, this building became an American Legion post as a joint venture of Chinese-American and Japanese-American war veterans; it was called the Cathay Post after a city in China. Today the name has been changed to Nisei #185 and is primarily an American Legion Club for Japanese-Americans. Nisei means second-generation.

This building once housed a bordello run by Jennie Holmes and other madams. Madams at many parlors such as this one openly sent invitations to gentlemen to solicit their business. According to Forbes Parkhill, a Denver newspaperman and historian, at least one marriage dissolved when a wife discovered her husband's hand-addressed invitation among his possessions.

The madams mailed engraved invitations to their opening soirees, which were elegant events where champagne

American Legion Cathay Post/Nisei Post #185. This photo was taken in 1928, when the building was used by the Chinese Masonic Lodge. — *Denver Public Library, Western History Department*

flowed freely. Madams also had business cards printed, often ordered from prestigious stores such as Daniels and Fisher, to solicit business. Some of the cards were subtle:

Veronica Baldwin
2020 Market Street
Phone Main 2250 Denver, Co

Others were openly suggestive:

Salome Club
(Miss Helen Roth)
1909–11 Market
When out for a good time stop at "The Salome Club"

In 1892, the madams printed a "Red Book" for the Knights Templar Convention that advertised their wares. Advertisements such as these were printed:

Jennie Holmes, 23 rooms — 3 parlors, 2 ball rooms and pool room and 15 boarders. Everything correct — Choice wines

Blanche Brown at 20th - Markets
Lots of Boarders
"All the comforts of Home"

Early brothels in Denver received gold dust as payment. Later it was common for patrons to purchase tokens from the madams to pay women for their services. This system allowed the madams to maintain a tight rein on cash transactions.

⑨ MATTIE SILKS HOUSE
2009 Market Street
Denver Landmark designation

Mattie, once the "Queen of The Row," came to Denver in the summer of 1876 and bought this house of pleasure in the late 1870s. She rented it to other madams and sold it to a competitor, Jennie Rogers, for $4,600 in January 1880.

From the outside brothels often resembled typical family dwellings. This 1890's photograph shows 1906-14 Market Street. After these buildings were demolished, Fire House #5 was erected on this site in 1923. — *Denver Public Library, Western History Department.*

Jennie stayed here for a few years, and then the house passed into the hands of several different madams until the reform movement shut down all the brothels.

Over the years, Mattie operated several houses on Market Street. The best known of these were at 1942 and 1916 Market. The latter house she ran for 56 years either as a brothel or, after reform, as the Silks Hotel. Her personal residence was in Curtis Park at 2635 Lawrence Street, which she bought in 1880. She died on January 7, 1929, at the age of 83 and is buried under the name of Martha A. Ready at Fairmount Cemetery. Mattie went through several fortunes in her lifetime and died with an estate of $6,500. After probate expenses, her heirs were left with a mere $2,000.

Over the years, the streets and lots of this neighborhood have changed. The streets grew from dirt paths to brick-paved thoroughfares and then asphalt-covered roads.

Amenities such as sidewalks and lighting were added. These improvements carved into the building lots. This building, which once was on the third lot from the corner, now appears much closer to the intersection.

Cross Twentieth Street and stand on the corner of Twentieth and Market streets.

⑩ HOUSE OF MIRRORS
1942 Market Street

The best-known maison de joie on Market Street was the infamous House of Mirrors, built by Jennie Rogers in 1888 on property acquired from Minnie Clifford, another madam on the street. When Jennie opened her new parlor house, she surpassed Mattie Silks as the "Queen of The Row." According to Forbes Parkhill, this had always been her goal, as she told her boyfriend, "I'd sell my soul, if any, for a house finer than Mattie's." The House of Mirrors was a good example of the opulence of the bordellos in the tenderloin. It had a billiard room, ballroom, bar, and a dining room where only the best food and liquor were sold. The girls wore the latest high-fashion clothing, for which they were often charged more than the retail price by local merchants, who knew they could get away with it. At 1942 Market Street there were floor-to-ceiling mirrors and mirrors

The House of Mirrors, when it was used for the Buddhist Mission. Notice the changes that were made to the roof line and facade when this building was converted to a warehouse in 1948. The aging brick was plastered with stucco to preserve it.
— *Colorado Historical Society*

The House of Mirrors, a former brothel, with remnants of its gracious past. The interior included elaborate mirrors and woodwork. This photo was taken after 1919, during the time that it was used by the Buddhist Mission. — *Colorado Historical Society*

on the ceilings surrounded with fine woods such as bird's-eye maple and mahogany.

The House of Mirrors was so successful that Jennie almost immediately needed to expand. She leased the building next door at 1946 Market Street and created a brothel with a Turkish harem theme. She also owned 1950 Market Street. Jennie died of Bright's disease on October 17, 1909. She is buried at Fairmount under the name Leah J. Wood. Jennie left an estate of $200,000, including Denver real estate and bonds. She was considered the most beautiful madam on The Row. At Jennie's death, Mattie Silks not only regained her title as "Queen of The Row," but also quickly purchased the House of Mirrors from Jennie's estate.

Tombstone of Jennie Rogers, the "most beautiful madam on The Row," at Fairmount Cemetery. She is buried under the name Leah J. Wood. — *Randy Brown Photographer*

In 1919, T. Ono, reverend of the Buddhist Mission of North America, purchased this property from Mattie Silks. The Buddhist Mission was established in Denver in 1916 at 1950 Lawrence Street. The mission used a property at 1917 Market Street in 1917 and 1918 and moved to the House of Mirrors in 1919. The property was officially transferred to the Buddhist Mission in 1929. In 1948, when the property was converted to a warehouse, the beautiful bird's-eye maple was removed and donated to the Sigma Chi fraternity house at the University of Denver by Dr. Nolie Mumey. This paneling was destroyed by a fire at the Sigma Chi house in 1979.

5 LIZZIE PRESTON'S "HOUSE"
1943 Market Street

This parlor house was the scene of a well-publicized scandal. On a March evening in 1880, Elizabeth "Baby" Doe, with a police escort, raided the premises of Lizzie Preston, a well-known madam, to catch her husband in an indelicate situation and obtain grounds for her divorce from Harvey Doe. This freed her to marry the very wealthy, but married, silver king Horace Tabor after his equally scandalous divorce from his first wife, Augusta. Tabor made his fortune in Leadville by outfitting miners and gaining a percentage of their digs. He was appointed for a short term to fill a U.S. Senate vacancy and married Baby Doe while in Washington, D.C. After the silver crash of 1893, he lost his fortune. Baby Doe and Horace lost their Capitol Hill mansion, at 1260 Sherman Street, moved to the mountains for a time, and then returned to Denver in 1898 when he was appointed postmaster for the city of Denver. He died a year later.

When Market Street was a red-light district, it was also occupied by saloons and gambling establishments. Popular forms of gambling were horse and foot races, faro, stud poker, keno, monte, billiards, black jack, and roulette.

⓫ EL CHAPULTEPEC
1962 Market Street or 1320 Twentieth Street

Built in the late 1880s, this structure once housed saloons, cribs, and gambling. The restaurant El Chapultepec was named for a park on an imposing rocky site just south of Mexico City. It was the first point occupied in the Valley of Mexico by the Aztecs and was developed as a playground for the last Aztec emperors. The building has been owned by the Romero family since 1929. When it first opened as a restaurant/bar in 1933, it featured mariachi music; now it is one of the foremost jazz clubs in the country. Over the years, such well-known personalities as Woody Herman, Harry Cox, Chet Baker, Red Holloway, Herb Ellis, Slide Hampton, Branford Marsalis, and Al Pike have appeared here.

Walk to the intersection of Twentieth Street and Larimer Street.

LARIMER STREET

Larimer Street was named after William Larimer, the leader of a group of men who came to Denver on November 16, 1858, from Lawrence, Kansas. They took over the claim of the St. Charles group and changed the

Examples of the late nineteenth- and early twentieth-century buildings that are common north of Twentieth Street on Larimer Street. In this photo, the building on the left is the Western Beef Building, next to it is the American Inn, and the building at the right end is Johnnie's Market. Ed Maestas, owner of Johnnie's and unofficial mayor of NoDo, remembers Larimer as "one of the busiest streets in Denver." This single block boasted a Safeway, a J. C. Penney, two drug stores, and six small grocery stores. — *Randy Brown Photographer*

Looking south from Twentieth Street on Larimer. Notice the results of the Skyline Urban Renewal Project. — *Randy Brown Photographer*

settlement's name to Denver City. Larimer named most of the streets in this part of Denver. He claimed to have built the first dwelling in Denver City, at the southeast corner of Fifteenth and Larimer streets. He lobbied for public office twice, lost both times, and left Denver in four years after having done well speculating in Denver real estate.

Larimer Street has a rich ethnic heritage. People of Italian, Polish, Jewish, Japanese, Hispanic, and African-American background all have called it home. "This is where immigrants centered their lives and where Denver had a true mix of cultures," said Karle Seydel, executive director of the North Larimer Business District. People not only worked here but also lived in the neighborhood above their businesses or in rented rooms. Mabel Googins, director of Tamai Towers in Sakura Square, said, "There was a special ambiance here. Everyone knew everybody." The residential feeling in the neighborhood changed in the early 1960s with a zoning ordinance affecting the venting of cooking stoves. Most property owners declined to spend the money needed to bring their buildings up to code and instead closed off the living quarters or used them only for storage.

Despite this, the strength of Larimer Street is still in its diversity of people. According to Ed Maestas of Johnnie's Market, "I'd rather be here than any other place in Denver. People here are what they are." And what they are ranges from street people to business executives.

Nowhere are the extremes of downtown Denver's past and present more obvious than at the corner of Twentieth and Larimer streets. The Skyline Urban Renewal Project, which rebuilt thirty blocks between Twentieth Street and Speer Boulevard and between Curtis and Larimer streets, was approved in 1967 after many of the area's businesses moved uptown or to the suburbs. The moves left many vacant buildings, flophouses and bars, and it was felt that urban renewal was the answer. If you look to the south you will see the results. Twenty-seven new complexes were built under this project, beginning in 1971 with the Prudential Plaza Building and concluding in 1984 with the Tabor Center development. Look north and see how Denver's past is reflected.

Many of the buildings to the north are more than 100 years old. La Popular at 2012 Larimer Street was built in 1891. Western Beef at 2048 Larimer Street, the American Inn at 2046 Larimer Street, and the Turre Building, with its interesting turret, at 2063 Larimer Street, were all built in 1880.

Larimer Street from Twentieth Street to Twenty-third Street is designated as a Neighborhood Business Revitalization Zone. As much as 50 percent of a commercial renovation or construction project's cost may be financed by the Mayor's Office of Economic Development at a negotiated interest rate.

The North Larimer Business District runs from Nineteenth Street to Broadway, encompassing an area from

Rendering of the restored Western Beef and American Inn buildings. Shown is a plan that converts the structures into nightclubs and office space. — *Murphy-Stevens Architects*

Murals by artist J. Castillo, adorning the walls of La Casa De Manuel. The painted shields show the sources of ingredients in Mexican food. — *Randy Brown Photographer*

The Stanley K. Yoshimura family in its SKY Home Bakery, at 2151 Larimer Street, in the 1950s. Yoshimura was a pastry chef for the Brown Palace Hotel before opening his own bakery and coffee shop. The "SKY" in the bakery's name are his initials. — *Youko Yamasaki/Miyuki Mabel Googins*

Wynkoop Street to Curtis Street. The district holds a fund-raiser called Fiesta Fiesta in August that celebrates not only the Hispanic heritage of the neighborhood, but also all other ethnic groups. The North Larimer Business District started in 1987 with seven members and had grown to 50 by 1994.

◆4 THE THORNDYKE/BURLINGTON HOTEL
2201 Larimer Street
Denver Landmark Designation

Knox, Currier, and Weicker obtained a building permit for this structure, then known as the Thorndyke, in 1890. It became the Burlington Hotel in 1901. The building was designed by Frank Edbrooke, Colorado's second licensed architect. Edbrooke also designed the Navarre (Museum of Western Art) in 1800, the Oxford Hotel in 1891, the Brown Palace Hotel in 1892. Frank came to Denver in August of 1879 to supervise the construction of the Tabor Block and continued his practice here until he retired in 1914. His father, Robert J was a structural and mechanical engineer. Frank and his brothers, Willoughby J. and George, who also became well known architects, learned their trade by helping their father rebuild much of Chicago after its great fire in 1871.

This building was probably constructed as an apartment hotel, where people had their

Larimer Street, looking north from Twenty-first Street in the early 1950s, showing the Burlington Hotel in the background. Karle Seydel, executive director of the North Larimer Business District, said the goal today is to turn the area into an international market-place. — *Youko Yamasaki/Miyuki Mabel Googins*

Computer rendering of a Denver Landmark, showing the architect's plan for the renovated Burlington Hotel, originally designed by well-known Denver architect Frank Edbrooke. The arched entry is typical of Edbrooke's work. — *Murphy-Stevens Architects*

Detail of the Burlington Hotel's entry, typical of the special features of Denver's older buildings. — *Randy Brown Photographer*

permanent residences. In its early years it was not listed in city directories under hotels, and when you enter the building there is no lobby, only a vestibule and a stairway leading to many small rooms. The 30,000-square-foot building has a U-shaped design, with a narrow light well in the center. The main floor was used for retail establishments.

Like north Larimer Street in general, the Burlington is in transition. It was once a beautiful building, then was neglected and became dilapidated, and now it is being renovated.

5 CHRISTOPHER COLUMBUS HALL/EL BRONCO BAR
2219 Larimer Street

This building, completed in 1888, is said to be one of the oldest bars in Denver still located at its original site. The old name reflects the Italian heritage of its first owners. It is first listed as the El Bronco Bar in the 1970 directory. It retains its original tin ceiling, which is mostly hidden under a modern drop ceiling.

CHRISTOPHER COLUMBUS HALL,

A CHOICE LINE OF

Wines, Liquors and Cigars,

ALSO DEALER IN

Imported Maccaroni, Cheese and Olive Oils.

2219 Larimer Street,

DENVER, - - COLORADO.

I drink at Christopher Columbus Hall. **SIRO MANGINI, Prop.** I don't, but will.

Early advertisement for the Columbus Hall, 2219 Larimer Street. — *Colorado Historical Society*

6 SACRED HEART CHURCH
2760 Larimer Street
Denver Landmark designation

Built in 1879 by Bishop Joseph Machebeuf, this is the oldest church building continuously in use in Denver. At one time, a convent and a school were associated with the church; the nearby school building is now used as a parish center and the convent is now Sacred Heart House, a refuge for single women and families. Among the church's early parishioners were Molly Brown and Baby Doe Tabor. Horace Tabor, who had recently joined the Catholic Church, received the last rites on his death bed at the Windsor Hotel from a priest of Sacred Heart Church, and his requiem mass was celebrated here. The iron fence around the rectory on the corner of Twenty-eighth Street and Larimer Street is from the Tabor mansion on Sherman Street.

Now painted yellow, Sacred Heart Church originally was unpainted sandstone and brick. When it was built, the church's steeple was six feet taller than today and was a landmark for travelers. In 1911, a fire in the building caused the sanctuary to be moved. The original stained-glass windows remain. The parish is working to renovate the church's interior, including murals that were painted over in the 1950s and are being replaced with new murals.

12 QUAKER HOTEL
2000 Larimer Street

This building was once a hotel, but later, as with so many hotels in this area, it became a flophouse. The Kentucky Liquor and Wine Company was on the first floor from 1895 to 1913, when it moved to 1757 Lawrence Street. The tavern in this building has a unique square bar in

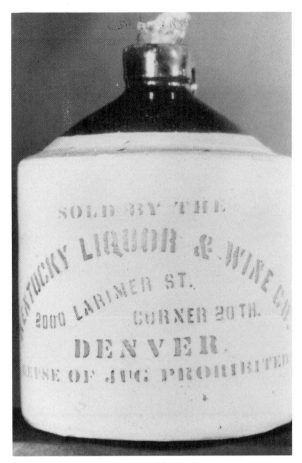

Kentucky Liquor & Wine Co. was located at 2000 Larimer Street and 2002 Larimer Street from 1895 to 1913, when it moved to 1757 Lawrence Street. Liquor was sold in ceramic jugs like this one. — *Colorado Historical Society*

the center. Be sure to notice the tin cornices around the building's roof line.

Follow Twentieth Street toward Lawrence Street and stop at the alley behind the Quaker Hotel.

Interior of Sacred Heart Church, built in 1879. — *Denver Public Library, Western History Department*

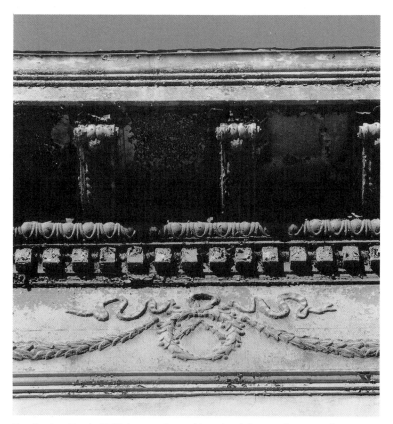

The Quaker Hotel, 2000 Larimer Street. Note the elaborate design work on its metal cornice. — *Randy Brown Photographer*

Interior of a Larimer Street Saloon prior to 1916, when Colorado went dry.
— *Colorado Historical Society*

13 KOPPER HOTEL/AIREDALE HOTEL
1215–19 Twentieth Street

This building was constructed in 1889 as the Kopper Hotel by Alfred Kopper, who came to Denver in 1882 for his step-daughter's health. (Notice the Kopper Hotel sign on the alley wall.) In 1919 the facade was changed when it became the Airedale Hotel. Notice the name and date on the Twentieth Street side.

Continue to the corner of Twentieth Street and Lawrence Street.

LAWRENCE STREET

Charles A. Lawrence was one of the "men from Lawrence," Kansas, who arrived with William Larimer in November 1858, and settled the Denver City side of Cherry Creek. He was here from 1858 to 1860 and built his first cabin where the northeast corner of Fifteenth Street and Lawrence Street now lies. He was an officer of Arapahoe County, in the Kansas Territory and Jefferson Territory. Lawrence also was a vestry man of St. John's Church in the Wilderness.

7 AINSWORTH BUILDING
2151 Lawrence Street

William Ainsworth moved to Denver in 1877. He was a watch and clockmaker who was known for his precision, and he is reputed to have been the first person to use aluminum, beginning in the 1880s. His company also designed, built, and repaired bank vaults and compasses, and in 1943 created a pocket transit for which it gained national recognition. The company won awards for its rifle sights, used by the military in both World Wars, and it worked on a precision instrument for the atomic bomb in World War II. This building has had at least five additions, starting with the original building in the alley in 1886 and continuing through the 1940s. The tower in the center of this complex was designed to give the height required for a plumb line to test the accuracy of delicate analytical balances. It is also rumored that spots on the Daniels and Fisher Tower at Sixteenth and Arapahoe streets were used to calibrate rifle sights from the Ainsworth Tower.

Turn right on Lawrence Street and head toward Nineteenth Street.

The Ainsworth Building, with its unusual tower. The tower can be seen more easily from a distance than at close range. — *Randy Brown Photographer*

14 TRI-STATE BUDDHIST TEMPLE
1947 Lawrence Street

With the construction of this structure in 1947, the Buddhist Mission of North America has completed a full circle. The mission was established near here in 1916 at 1950 Lawrence Street; it moved to 1917 and 1942 Market Street; it returned here in 1947 and became the Tri-State Buddhist Temple in 1976. The temple originally served Colorado, Nebraska, and Wyoming, but now also includes New Mexico, Texas, Oklahoma, and Kansas.

Most early Japanese residents of this area arrived around the turn of the century to work in agriculture and railroading. In 1916, when the Buddhist Mission was organized, it had 850 members from Colorado and Nebraska. The largest populations came from the city of Denver and from agricultural communities in both states. This building was dedicated in 1949 over a four-day span. Its funding was facilitated by the large numbers of Japanese who settled here after being interned at camps in Colorado or otherwise relocated during World War II.

In addition to being a place of worship, the temple serves as a social center, credit union, school, and gymnasium for the Japanese community, where the Japanese can learn about or stay in touch with various aspects of their Buddhist heritage.

The facade of the temple was redesigned in the 1970s to fit in with the neighboring Sakura Square development.

Continue up Lawrence Street to Nineteenth Street, turn right, and enter Sakura Square at Nineteenth and Larimer streets.

15 SAKURA SQUARE

This development, part of the Skyline Urban Renewal Project, was designed to fit around the Buddhist temple built 23 years before. The land for Sakura Square was acquired from the Denver Urban Renewal Authority for $188,000 in 1970, and the development opened in 1972. Sakura is the Japanese word for cherry blossom, and each June this is the site of a Cherry Blossom Festival, where Japanese crafts and storytelling are taught and shared.

Sakura Square sits at the heart of Denver's old Japanese community, where people both worked and resided. The businesses here ranged from the professions to bakeries, groceries, clothing stores, restaurants, barber shops, and hotels. All of this was torn down in the Skyline project to make way for Sakura Square.

Inside the square you will see:

◆ Tamai Towers, the tall building in the rear, is a retirement community. It is named for Reverend Tamai, who was minister for the Buddhist Mission of North America for 53 years. It is delightful to find this oasis in the center of urban sprawl, and it is just one of the many residential towers downtown. In 1994, there were at least 2,800 people living downtown.

◆ The Japanese shrine titled the Tower of Compassion, in the gardens outside the Sakura Square buildings.

◆ A bust of Minoru Yasui, who was an attorney and director of Denver's Commission on Community Relations. A community-service award of $2,000, funded by local foundations and corporations, is given eleven months a year in his name. The recipients donate this honorarium to charities of their choice.

◆ A bust of Colorado Governor Ralph Carr, who served as governor from 1939 to 1943. He is honored here by the Japanese because he welcomed Japanese-Americans to

The Tower of Compassion, a Japanese shrine at Sakura Square, with the Tamai Towers in the background. — *Randy Brown Photographer*

Colorado during World War II, an unpopular position that may have doomed his future political career.

Take another look at the beautiful Japanese gardens as you exit Sakura Square and walk back to the corner of Nineteenth and Lawrence streets. Proceed toward the intersection of Eighteenth and Lawrence streets.

16 J. P. DUNN BUILDING
1825 Lawrence Street

This structure was built for J.P. Dunn in 1912. In 1923, the J.P. Dunn Shoe and Leather Company and the J.P. Dunn Tire Western Shoe and Rubber Company which had been in business in Denver since 1888 located here. The two companies occupied this site until 1973. The building was designed by Robert Willison and Montana Fallis. Willison came to Denver in 1883 and also designed the City Auditorium Theatre in 1908 and St. Cajetan's church in Auraria in 1926. Montana Fallis worked for Frank Edbrooke and in 1898 established his architectural practice. He designed the Oxford Annex, which is also on this tour, in 1912.

EIGHTEENTH STREET

Numbered streets became major thoroughfares of the city after the railroad came to Denver. The 1400, 1500, and 1600 blocks of Eighteenth Street are part of the Lower Downtown Historic District.

⑰ DENVER CITY CABLE RAILWAY COMPANY/ SPAGHETTI FACTORY
1801 Lawrence Street/1215 Eighteenth Street
National Register and Denver Landmark designations

Built in 1889 for the Denver City Cable Railway Company, this building originally had a dirt floor in the basement and a two-story-high steam boiler that was used to power the cables that pulled trolley cars along the street. The chimney as it exists today is actually shorter than the original, because seven feet fell off during a windstorm. When the building opened, it was the largest street-car cable plant in the world. The fare was only five cents when the line opened. From the 1920s into the 1950s, this structure was used as a parking garage.

Denver City Cable Railway Company. Many changes were made to this 1889 building after this photograph was taken, including additional windows, the recessed corner, and a smokestack that is approximately seven feet shorter than its original height. — *Denver Public Library, Western History Department*

As you walk by the alley behind the City Cable Railway Company Building, notice the bolts on the red brick. They indicate the use of tie-rod construction that predates the use of steel girders. The rods went from one end of the building to the other; usually the front end was tied off with a decorative plate and the alley side was bolted off. With this type of construction, building heights usually did not exceed five stories.

8 ▶ GUMRY HOTEL
1725-1733 Lawrence Street

This hotel, which is no longer standing, was built in 1887 by Peter Gumry, a contractor who arrived in Denver in 1862 and was later the superintendent of construction at the state Capitol. This was the site of the worst hotel disaster in Denver's history, when a boiler explosion around midnight on an August night in 1895 destroyed the building, killing twenty-two people, among them Peter Gumry. The explosion caused damage for two blocks along Lawrence and Larimer streets. Following an investigation into the causes of the disaster, the city's regulations for steam boilers were stiffened.

Catty-corner from the Gumry was the Markham Hotel, where many visiting players stayed during Denver's early days of baseball. Asa Brainard, star pitcher for the 1869 Cincinnati Reds, moved to Denver in 1883 and lived at the Markham. Brainard served as the hotel detective and ran its pool hall, and he died at the hotel in 1888.

Walk down Eighteenth Street to its junction with Larimer Street. Long-time Denverites hold fond memories of the elegant buildings that once stood at this corner but are now gone. Their demise was hastened by a change in Denver's height restriction in 1953. Until then, most buildings in Denver, with a few exceptions, were limited to twelve stories. Once this height limit was removed, the buildings at this intersection and others like

126

Windsor Hotel. The junction of Eighteenth and Larimer streets once anchored a small-business and residential neighborhood. This early photo of the Windsor Hotel shows the neighborhood in transition, with unpaved streets and frame buildings.
— *Denver Public Library, Western History Department*

them met with competition from Denver's new skyscrapers. The buildings lost their tenants to newer and larger structures and thus their death knell was sounded.

6 WINDSOR HOTEL
Northeast corner of Larimer and Eighteenth streets

The Windsor Hotel opened on June 23, 1880, and immediately became known as a hotel without comparison west of the Mississippi River. The hotel originated with the frustration of a young Scotsman named James Duff who could not find adequate housing in Denver in the 1870s because of the rapid population growth brought on by the coming of the railroad. He was part of a group of English investors — The Denver Mansions Company — who decided to build a hotel with "no expense spared" to meet this need. The building was described in newspapers as "proud and elegant." It had 300 guest rooms, some of which were combined into suites, a billiard room, a suspended ballroom, steam heating, walnut furniture, diamond-dust mirrors, and elegant dining. When the hotel opened it had the best liquor list in Denver, and Harry H. Tammen was head bartender. Tammen later owned many curio shops in Denver and co-founded The Denver Post with Frederick Bonfils. Later in the Windsor's life, 3,000 silver dollars were laid in its barroom floor. Famous people who stayed here included Presidents Grant, Cleveland, Taft, and Teddy Roosevelt, as well as Oscar Wilde, Rudyard Kipling, Mark Twain, Buffalo Bill, John L. Sullivan, and W.H. Vanderbilt. Horace and Baby Doe Tabor started their married lives together here in the bridal suite, and Tabor's life ended in Room 302.

Interior shots of the elaborate Windsor Hotel, built in 1880. At its opening, it was thought to be the fanciest hotel west of the Mississippi River. When it was closed and readied for demolition in 1959, its lush furnishings were auctioned off. The building was torn down in 1960. — *Colorado Historical Society*

7 DUFF BLOCK
Southwest corner of Eighteenth and Larimer streets

This office building was named for and built by James Duff, who was the on-site manager of the Denver Mansions Company. While he was in Denver, Duff served on the boards of the Colorado National Bank and The Denver Club. To call something the Duff Block or the Barclay Block did not mean that the building took up the entire city block, but that it was an impressive building.

8 BARCLAY BLOCK
Southeast corner of Eighteenth and Larimer streets

This building, constructed in 1884, also was built by James Duff and was named after one of his partners, James Barclay, another Scotsman. Beginning in 1884, the Barclay Block served as the last private site of the state executive offices and legislature prior to the construction of the state Capitol. The legislature started moving out of Barclay in the fall of 1894 and began to use the new Capitol in January 1895.

In the Barclay's basement were the famous Windsor Baths, with a sudatorium built of marble, polished hardwood, and stained glass, a shampooers' hall, a swimming bath, and a cooling room. There also were Turkish, Russian, Roman, and electric baths primed by two artesian wells that were said to be the deepest and purest in the world. The hours between seven in the morning and noon were reserved for ladies. The baths' motto was "Cleanliness and Thoroughness and Politeness." It was advertised as "preventing poisonous ferments in the body." The Barclay Block was demolished in 1971.

Duff Block, built by the Denver Mansions Company of England, which was headed in Denver by James Duff. Duff also was involved with building the Windsor Hotel and Barclay Block. Notice the trolley tracks and the street lighting. — *Denver Public Library, Western History Department*

Detail of a modern street light in the Lower Downtown Historic District, showing how it reflects earlier lights, as seen in the previous picture of the Duff Block. — *Randy Brown Photographer*

A later photo of the intersection of Eighteenth and Larimer streets, depicting the Barclay Block. Notice that the street lights have changed again. This style is also copied in today's downtown street lights.
— *Denver Public Library, Western History Department*

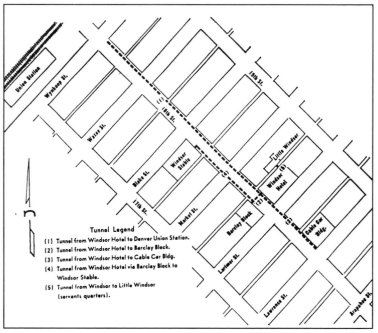

Tunnel Legend

(1) Tunnel from Windsor Hotel to Denver Union Station.
(2) Tunnel from Windsor Hotel to Barclay Block.
(3) Tunnel from Windsor Hotel to Cable Car Bldg.
(4) Tunnel from Windsor Hotel via Barclay Block to Windsor Stable.
(5) Tunnel from Windsor to Little Windsor (servants quarters).

Sketch of Lower Downtown Denver's historic tunnels, by Kenton Forrest and Charles Albi. Since this was drawn, they have done more research and found that the tunnels were under the sidewalks, not the streets. — *Kenton Forrest and Charles Albi, "Denver's Railroads," Colorado Railroad Museum, Golden*

Tunnels under the sidewalks led from the Windsor Hotel to the Baths, Union Station, and Windsor Stables to keep famous people sheltered from prying eyes and others from inclement weather. The tunnels later were used for storage and since have been mostly filled in.

Follow Larimer Street to Seventeenth Street past several urban-renewal projects. From the corner of Seventeenth and Larimer streets, step back ten feet and look at the D&F Tower, surrounded by the steel and glass of the Tabor Center.

◆ 9 D&F TOWER
National Register and Denver Landmark designation
AND TABOR CENTER
16th and Arapahoe

Until 1953, the Daniels and Fisher Tower was one of the tallest buildings in the downtown area, until the twelve-story height restriction was lifted. The tower was part of the old Daniels and Fisher store, the rest of which was lost to the Skyline Urban Renewal Project. The Tabor Center now sits on that store's property, Horace Tabor's Tabor Block, and other properties, and was the last project finished under Skyline Urban Renewal, in 1984. It includes the nineteen-story, 420-room Westin Hotel, the Shops at the Tabor Center, and the thirty-story One Tabor Center office complex.

Walk along Seventeenth Street to Market Street.

18 COLUMBIA HOTEL
1320–80 Seventeenth Street
Denver Landmark designation

Constructed as a commercial building circa 1872–1878, it was converted in 1892 to a hotel that had 90 guest rooms, hot and cold running water, steam heat, and electricity.

SEVENTEENTH STREET

All of Seventeenth Street from here to Union Station is incorporated in the Lower Downtown Historic District. Seventeenth Street once boasted more than ten hotels and was known as "The Wall Street of the West" because of the predominance of banking and financial institutions here.
Cross Market Street.

⑲ MARKET STREET STATION

Opened in 1983, this is one of the turnaround stations for the Sixteenth Street Mall shuttle, which traverses downtown to Civic Center Station. The lower level is for city buses. If you look across the street to the Columbia Hotel, the historic buildings connected to it are known as Market Center and have Denver Landmark status. Dates of construction for these buildings range from 1881 to 1893. Restoration of the five buildings into offices, restaurants, and shops was finished in 1980.

Continue along Seventeenth Street toward Union Station until you are standing in front of the Barth Hotel at the junction of Seventeenth and Blake streets.

⑳ UNION WAREHOUSE/BARTH HOTEL
1514 Seventeenth Street
National Register and Denver Landmark designations

This structure was built in 1882 as a warehouse for Moritz Barth by architect Frederick Carl Eberley. Eberley is also credited with having designed the tower building (1890-1891) of the Tivoli Brewery complex in Auraria. The Union Warehouse was converted in the late 1880s to the Union Hotel, which had 100 rooms. The name was changed to the Elk Hotel in 1905. (Notice the brass Elk Hotel nameplate in the sidewalk by the Seventeenth Street alley.)

Early interior shots of the Barth (formerly Union) Hotel. — *Denver Public Library, Western History Department*

New Union Hote

The Barth Hotel, a National Register and Denver Landmark building. This photo shows the building when it was the new Union Hotel, after its renovation from the Union Warehouse.
— *Denver Public Library, Western History Department*

Early photo of the Columbia Hotel, a Denver Landmark. Note the horse and wagon and the room rates.

— *Denver Public Library, Western History Department*

In 1931, the name was changed back to the Barth Hotel by Barth's son to honor his father. Today, the building holds 62 units of housing for senior citizens and is owned and operated by the non-profit Senior Housing Options Inc. which is a state licensed alternative care facility.

Cross Seventeenth Street toward Eighteenth Street, and then cross Blake Street so you are in front of the St. Elmo Building.

㉑ ST. ELMO HOTEL
1433 Seventeenth Street

In 1896, when this structure was built, hotels were not only for travelers; many people called them their permanent residences. Although the ground floor of this structure has been recessed to allow light in the basement, it originally extended to the full dimensions of the building. The belt of

The St. Elmo Hotel. Notice how the building's street-level appearance changed after this photo was taken, as the ground floor was recessed to obtain more natural light in the basement. Also note the signs on the building. — *Denver Public Library, Western History Department*

A 1937 photo of the Windsor Stables Building, now known as Blake Street Bath & Racquet Club. Notice the brick streets, details of which have been incorporated into the sidewalks and crosswalks of the Coors Field area and the Lower Downtown Historic District. — *Colorado Historical Society*

stonework on the second and third levels is reminiscent of that used in the design of Coors Field.

Walk up Blake Street toward Eighteenth Street.

22 WINDSOR STABLES BUILDING/WINDSOR OMNIBUS
& CARRIAGE COMPANY STABLES
1732–1772 Blake Street
Denver Landmark designation

Known today as the Blake Street Bath and Racquet Club, this building was constructed in 1881. Originally, there were stables in back of this whole block. During this period, stables and livery businesses were common all over the downtown area.

Cross Eighteenth Street.

㉓ G. E. Building
1441 Eighteenth Street
National Register designation

In this building, constructed in 1906, you can see the brick work with terra-cotta trim that is incorporated into the Coors Field design. Originally built as a site for processing metal, it served for many years as a General Electric warehouse and office complex.

㉔ Firehouse #5
1821 Blake Street

Look across the street at the building at 1821 Blake Street, which was constructed in 1896. In order to hold down expenses, the fire department used its own men to erect this structure. The home of the Denver Fire Department's

The G.E. Building. The company's sign remains on this building even though General Electric is no longer a tenant. Note, too, the terra-cotta trim. — *Randy Brown Photographer*

Firehouse #5, built in 1896 at 1821 Blake Street for Steam Company #5.
— *Randy Brown Photographer*

Steam Company #5, this unusual three-story firehouse had poles between each floor for the firemen to slide down. Firehouse #5 moved in 1923 to Nineteenth and Market streets and closed in 1973. Denver no longer has a commissioned fire station with the number 5.

In the days of horse-drawn fire wagons, the steam to pump water through firefighters' hoses was created by fires built under water filled metal containers in the wagons. As these wagons rushed to the rescue over rough dirt or brick streets, sparks from the fires under the containers flew out, causing disasters in some cases.

25 CROCODILOS II
1836 Blake Street

All of the exterior trim in the entry of this building has been salvaged from other buildings that have been demolished. Notice the pressed tin and the stone carvings. Decorative items such as these became popular on Denver buildings after the railroad made them easier to obtain from distant cities.

26 WINDSOR FARM DAIRY
1855–1865 Blake Street

This building was constructed in 1918 as a plant and warehouse for Windsor Farm Dairy. The dairy's cow pastures were located at Alameda Avenue and Dayton Street, now the site of Windsor Gardens, a retirement village. The processing for Windsor's dairy products was done in this building, and the dairy's motto was "Honest Milk from Clean Cows." The signage on this building is glazed terra cotta.

In 1928 H. Brown Cannon sold the company to Beatrice Foods. Mr. Cannon came to Denver in 1888 and worked at the Alameda Avenue farm and eventually became co-owner of the company with his partner Mike Penrose.

Beatrice sold its dairy products under the brand name Meadow Gold and after its acquisition of Windsor Farm Dairy moved Meadow Gold's processing facilities from the Ice House at 1801 Wynkoop Street to this building. Until this facility was closed, ice cream and milk were the main products produced here. Meadow Gold used this building until October 1972, when it moved the dairy processing operations to their current location in Englewood.

27 F. W. CROCKER AND COMPANY STEAM CRACKER FACTORY/NABISCO BUILDING
1852–1862 Blake Street
National Register designation

This building, known today as the Blake Street Terrace, has undergone many changes since its early days. It is on a site that has been home to cracker factories since the early 1870s. F. W. Crocker was involved in these early companies, and eventually the company took his name. His business was acquired by the American Biscuit Company in 1890 and became part of the National Biscuit Company in 1898. Some of the products available at the turn of the century were Denver Butters, Pearl Oysters, and Uneeda Bakers zwieback and graham crackers.

The present factory building was built after a fire in 1885. The center structure is new and was designed with narrow windows and arches to compliment the adjacent buildings. Peek in the alley to see how the new building fits in between two older structures. Nabisco occupied the building until 1942. At one time, many factories and industrial businesses were located in the downtown area, though this began to change in the 1940s.

Turn left down Nineteenth Street and walk to Wazee Street.

Windsor Farm Dairy Building, shown behind one of its early delivery wagons. The product line is listed on the wagon. — *Denver Public Library, Western History Department*

WAZEE STREET

Wazee is an Indian name selected for the street by William McGaa. The meaning of the word is unclear, but it may be a person's name. This street was the center of wholesale trade in Denver's early days. The 1700 to 1900 blocks on Wazee Street are all in the Lower Downtown Historic District.

28 WAZEE EXCHANGE
1523–1543 Nineteenth Street/1900 Wazee Street

Built in 1885 and expanded in 1890, this building was constructed as a wholesale grocery and mercantile center that supplied the railroads. The building's sandstone trim and gooseneck lamps were copied in parts of Coors Field.
Turn left and go down Wazee Street toward Seventeenth Street.

29 BEEBE & RUNYAN BUILDING
1863 Wazee Street

Designed by Montana Fallis and built in 1930, this 99,000-square-foot art-deco warehouse was the last major building constructed in lower downtown until after World War II. It is now a 47-unit loft development. The interior features terra-cotta tile walls and concrete pillars.

30 S & H SUPPLY
1732–1740 Wazee Street

Built in 1909, this structure features interesting corbeled cornices and brick panels on the exterior. The building was used in the 1920s as a garage for the Oxford Hotel and continued as a downtown parking garage into the 1950s.

The Beebe & Runyon Building. Like so many buildings in the downtown area, this warehouse has been converted into lofts, with modern-day amenities such as terrace decking. — *Randy Brown Photographer*

③① HENDRIE & BOLTHOFF
1743 Wazee Street
National Register designation

Built in 1907, this warehouse was designed by Frank E. Edbrooke. It was built for the Hendrie & Bolthoff Manufacturing and Supply Company, one of the leading mining machinery manufacturers for the West. Edbrooke also designed other buildings for Hendrie & Bolthof: a stable and wagon shed located at 19th and Inca and at 29th and Inca a warehouse and pipehouse. After starting business in Central City in 1861, Hendrie & Bolthoff moved to Denver in 1876 to be close to the transcontinental railroad, which had made Denver a major distribution center for the Rocky Mountain region. Because of the firm's success, Hendrie & Bolthoff eventually occupied most of this block, from here to

Seventeenth Street and from Wazee Street to Wynkoop Street. The company remained in LoDo until 1971.

Turn right at Seventeenth and Wazee streets and cross Seventeenth Street.

③② OXFORD HOTEL
1612 Seventeenth Street/1701 Wazee Street
National Register and Denver Landmark designations

The Oxford Hotel opened the first week of October 1891, with 400 rooms, steam heating, electric and gas lights, and some rooms with private bathrooms. Furnishings were antique oak and all rooms had outside windows. One could get a room in 1912 for $1, $1.50, or $2 per day. Fifty rooms were added in 1902, extending the building to the south on Wazee Street. One of the original owners was brewer Adolph Zang. Many well-known individuals stayed at

The Oxford Hotel, a National Register and Denver Landmark building, in a photo taken prior to 1933. Notice the exterior changes since this photo was taken. All of the doorways except the lobby door have been converted into windows. The Western Union office has since been changed to the Cruise Bar with its art-deco theme. — *Denver Public Library, Western History Department*

the Oxford Hotel, including Jack Demsey, Ernie Pyle, and presidents Warren G. Harding and Franklin Roosevelt.

This building was designed by Frank Edbrooke, who also designed the Denver Dry Goods Building in 1894 and the Masonic Building in 1889, Loretto Heights Academy in 1890 and 1891, and Central Presbyterian Church in 1892, along with the other buildings already mentioned. This hotel and all its rooms have been restored to the 1890s period, except for the art-deco Cruise Room, which is patterned after the lounge on the Queen Mary ocean liner. The Cruise Room was once the Western Union telegraph office, but it became a bar when prohibition was lifted in 1933. Colorado went dry in 1916, four years before the nation did, so the reversal had long been awaited.

The hotel's location near Union Station nurtured it throughout its existence, and when the railroads suffered their demise so did the hotel. It experienced a rebirth when Dana Crawford and Charles Calloway restored it in 1982 and 1983; the hotel reopened in June 1983 with 82 rooms. Crawford and Calloway have been among the primary forces in the revival of LoDo. Dana Crawford had a vision in 1965 for saving the city's heritage and using historic buildings at a time when the cry was tear down and rebuild. From her first redevelopment, the renewal of Larimer Square, she went on to restore the Oxford Hotel, the Ice House, and many other downtown landmarks. Be sure to go into the hotel to look at the wonderfully restored rooms and public areas.

33 Oxford Annex
1616 Seventeenth Street

In 1912, Montana Fallis and Robert Willison designed this second annex to the Oxford Hotel. Like the main building, the annex has a flower motif in its exterior design. The building was constructed on land owned by Struby

Estabrook, owners of the structure next door. Its rooms were smaller than those in the original hotel, to which it is connected by a passageway. It is thought to be the only glazed terra-cotta building left standing in the LoDo area. Note the HB at each corner of the building; the initials stand for Hamilton & Brooks Corporation, owner-managers of the Oxford Hotel at the time this addition was built.

34 STRUBY ESTABROOK BUILDING
1660 Seventeenth Street

This building was completed in 1886 for Fred F. Struby and George H. Estabrook as a warehouse and showroom for their wholesale grocery business, which had been located between Fifteenth and Sixteenth streets on Blake. Struby served as a director of the Colorado National Bank, and Estabrook's daughter, Mary, married Charles Kountze, the youngest of the Kountze brothers, who founded Colorado National Bank.

While Coors Field was being built, this building was home to the offices of the Denver Metropolitan Major League Baseball Stadium District. Its Colorado sandstone and rusticated stone are both incorporated in the stadium design.

WYNKOOP STREET

This street was named for Edward W. "Ned" Wynkoop, the first sheriff of Denver City. He was appointed by Governor James Denver of the Kansas Territory in November 1858. He was also one of the first shareholders of the Denver Town Company and a member of the St. Charles Company, an Indian agent, a member of the first regiment of the Colorado Volunteers, and an actor in early Denver theater productions.

After the coming of the train, this street became known as "warehouse row," and now sections of it have historic designation as a warehouse district. Much of this street used to be covered by railroad tracks, making walking extremely difficult. The 1700 and 1800 blocks of Wynkoop Street are in the Lower Downtown Historic District.

Cross Seventeenth Street at Wynkoop Street.

35 UNION DEPOT/UNION STATION
1700 Wynkoop Street
National Register and Denver Landmark designations

For more than 100 years, the focus of Seventeenth Street has been Union Station, originally called Union Depot.

Before the construction of Union Depot in 1881, there were many stations throughout the downtown area. In 1879, urged on by Jay Gould of the Union Pacific, the railroads agreed to consolidate the stations. The Union Depot and Railroad Company, headed by Walter S. Cheesman, purchased land between Sixteenth and Eighteenth streets on Wynkoop Street in 1879, and all of the railroads agreed that they would begin and end their passenger service at the new station. To meet the needs of the various companies, each set of tracks at Union Depot had three rails to allow for both narrow-gauge and standard-gauge traffic. When it opened to the public on June 1, 1881, this station was the largest building in Colorado and the largest train depot west of the Mississippi River. It had cost $405,000 to construct.

The building has changed over the years. In 1894, an electrical fire destroyed a large part of the center section of the main building. It was rebuilt and improved at a cost of $200,000. Between 1912 and 1914, the ownership changed and a new company, the Denver Union Terminal Railway Company, was formed to manage Union Station. This company decided to raze the 1894 central structure, and what you see today was built in 1914. Additional improvements have been made to the interior and exterior since then. Stone

A 1910 photo of the Welcome/Mizpah arch in front of the center section of Union Station, which was rebuilt after the 1894 fire. This arch was erected in 1906 and remained until 1931. It was illuminated by 1,600 light bulbs. — *Colorado Historical Society*

Photo of Seventeenth Street, ending with the first Union Depot, which lost its center section to fire in 1894. This photo was taken before the Oxford Hotel and the Struby Estabrook building were constructed, probably in the mid-1880s because the Denver City Railway Company building is shown. — *Colorado Historical Society*

for the sandstone wings of the station, the oldest parts of the structure, was quarried in the nearby towns of Morrison and Castle Rock.

If you enter the station and look at the wall over the ticket cage, you will see emblems of the railroad lines that formed the new ownership group. In addition to the station, the company owns fifteen acres of adjacent land between Sixteenth and Twentieth streets, and between Wynkoop and Delgany streets. Into the 1970s, there were tracks along many of the lower downtown streets and alleys to accommodate boxcars delivering to downtown businesses.

At its peak, 80 to 100 passenger trains a day ran through this station. In 1874, fares were comparable to stagecoach fares, charging ten cents a mile for short trips. A trip by either stagecoach or train to Cheyenne, Wyoming, would cost ten dollars. Union Station has greeted many

The last major change to the center section of Union Depot was its reconstruction in 1914. Notice the canopy and strong main entry, both of which are reflected in the design of Coors Field. This is now a National Register and Denver Landmark building. — *Randy Brown Photographer*

Detail shot of the canopy and supports at Union Station. — *Randy Brown Photographer*

dignitaries, including Presidents Harding, Wilson, Teddy and F. D. Roosevelt, Taft, Hoover, Eisenhower, and Truman. It has also been the setting for several movies and television shows, including the "Father Downing Mysteries" and "Perry Mason" programs, to name two.

An O-gauge model railroad set up in the basement has called Union Station its home for more than 60 years. It is open to the public, although viewing hours are limited.

36 DENVER CITY RAILWAY COMPANY BUILDING/
SHERIDAN HERITAGE
1635 Seventeenth Street
National Register and Denver Landmark designations

Known today as Streetcar Stables Lofts, this building was constructed in 1883 to house the horses and cars for the Denver City Railway Company. The location was chosen for its proximity to the new Union Depot, so people could get to and from the train easily. The trolley cars were stored

DINNER

(Served from 4:00 P. M. to 8:30 P. M.)

Choice of:
Cream of Green Asparagus Soup   or   Clear Consomme
Chilled Juices—Prune, Tomato or Grapefruit
Fruit Cup   Marinated Herring
Jumbo Shrimp Cocktail—30c Extra

TODAY'S SALAD
Combination Salad
French or Russian Dressing, Mayonnaise

ENTREES
(Price of Entree Determines Cost of Dinner)

Spaghetti and Meat Balls..1.25
Fried Deep Sea Scallops, Cocktail Sauce..............................1.25
Braised Veal Chops, Chasseur...1.40
Baked Sugar-cured Ham, Sauce Reine Marie.............................1.50
Roast Stuffed Duck, Sage Dressing....................................1.65
Chef's Pot Roast of Beef, Noodles, Own Gravy.........................1.40
Grilled Pork Chops on Toast, Apple Sauce.............................1.40
French Fried Jumbo Shrimp, Cocktail Sauce............................1.50
Grilled Lamb Chops, Mint Jelly.......................................1.50
One-half Farm Fresh Fried Young Chicken, Country Gravy
(30 minutes to cook)...1.50
Pan Fried Colorado Mountain Trout, Maitre d'Hotel....................1.60
T-Bone Steak 1.65
Broiled 12-ounce New York Cut Sirloin Steak au Natural...............2.25

Genuine Rye Bread   Dinner Rolls   Hot Muffins

POTATOES and VEGETABLES
Choice of Two:
Shoestring Potatoes   or   Au Gratin Potatoes
Baked Squash   or   Buttered Wax Beans

Chili Bowl 25

DESSERTS
Choice of:
Tango Cherries, Strawberry, Chocolate or Pineapple Sundae
Ice Cream   Orange Sherbet
Apple Sauce   Peach in Syrup   Fruit Jello
Fresh Strawberry or Chocolate Parfait—15c Extra
Fruit or Cream Pies 15   Cake Slice 10

Choice of:
Coffee   Hot Tea   (Milk or Buttermilk 10)

We Serve a Complete Line of Mixed Cocktails, Liquors, Beer and Wines

UNION STATION RESTAURANT   **Denver, Colorado**

Wednesday, November 2, 1949

A 1949 Union Station Restaurant menu. With the revitalization of the neighborhood, restaurants have returned to Union Station area, but, unfortunately, not with the same prices. — Denver Union Terminal Railway Company

A 1937 photo of Wynkoop Street, from Seventeenth Street to Eighteenth streets, showing the Hendrie & Bolthoff Building, the Spice Warehouse and Commission House, and the J. S. Brown Mercantile Building. The Seventeenth Street exterior to the Hendrie & Bolthoff (Denver City Railway Company) building exhibits the false front added by Mr. Sheridan. — *Colorado Historical Society*

Star on the Wynkoop Street side of the Sheridan Heritage building, indicating it was built with tie-rods instead of steel beams. These decorative plates, often found on a building's front, were shaped like stars, crescents, circles, rectangles, or fleurs-de-lis. — *Randy Brown Photographer*

Alley view of the Denver City Railway Company/Sheridan Heritage Building, showing the blending of old and new, with the tie-rod bolts of the original structure and the terraces added in the 1990s for loft living. — *Randy Brown Photographer*

Denver City Railway Company Building, a National Register building, in the mid-1880s before the false front was added. At the time, this building was home to horses and horse-drawn trolleys. — *Colorado Historical Society*

on the first floor along with a waiting room and offices, and the horses were stabled mainly on the second and third floors, with the attic used for grain storage. At the end of 1883, the company had fifteen and one-half miles of tracks, 200 horses, and 100 employees. The building was purchased by Mr. Sheridan in 1892 after cable and electric cars replaced the horse-drawn cars and the railway company merged into another. Sheridan added the false front on Seventeenth Street. Hendrie & Bolthoff bought the building in 1902 and stayed here until 1971. Now it has been converted to residential lofts and a restaurant and stores.

When you look at the Wynkoop side of the building, notice the stars on its facade, which indicate its pre-steel, tie-rod construction. If you feel like walking around to the alley on Seventeenth Street, you will notice a sharp contrast between the 1880s tie rods secured by bolts and the 1990s terrace additions for the lofts.

Old bricks showing through the asphalt on Eighteenth Street between Union Station and the Ice House. — *Randy Brown Photographer*

37 SPICE WAREHOUSE & COMMISSION HOUSE/EDWARD W.
WYNKOOP BUILDING
1738–1742 Wynkoop Street
Denver Landmark designation

Henry Stone purchased this land from J. S. Brown in
1899 and built this structure between 1899 and 1901 for a
spice warehouse and commission house. A commission
house brokered spices from suppliers to businesses and individuals; it was sometimes called a futures commission
merchant or wire house, and today would be known as a
brokerage firm. Stone's business occupied this site until
1922, when he leased it to his neighbor, the J. S. Brown
Mercantile Group.
Walk along Wynkoop Street toward Eighteenth Street.

38 J. S. BROWN MERCANTILE BUILDING
1634 Eighteenth Street
National Register designation

This building was constructed in 1899 for the leading
wholesale dealer of grocery and related products west of
Chicago, supplying Colorado and much of New Mexico,
Utah, and Wyoming. J. S. Brown Mercantile was started in
Denver in 1861. John Sidney Brown was one of the directors
of the Board of Trade that was organized in 1867 to aid in
construction of the Denver Pacific Railroad. He also was
instrumental in acquiring the land for Union Depot.
The J. S. Brown Mercantile Building is one of the few
examples left in LoDo of a mercantile showroom where all
of the original pressed tin ceilings, oak trim, and maple
floors still exist. The building now contains a brew pub,
nightclub, billiard hall, and residential lofts. These improvements were made from 1988 to 1991.
Cross Eighteenth Street.

39 BDT BUILDING/ATRIUM BUILDING
1621 Eighteenth Street

Built in 1919 on land once owned by the Littleton Creamery, this building was designed by Fisher and Fisher and constructed for Burke, Donaldson and Taylor. (Notice their initials near the roof on the Wynkoop Street and Eighteenth Street sides of the building.) This building was constructed as a wholesale produce warehouse. Look inside and see how well the decor of the period, including slate floors and tiles, has been incorporated into the new office design. The original timber construction of this building was refinished and left exposed.

40 LITTLETON CREAMERY/BEATRICE FOODS/
THE ICE HOUSE
1801 Wynkoop Street
National Landmark designation

The corner structure was built in 1903 by the Littleton Creamery. This company started business in 1886 as a wholesaler of dairy products and a vendor of dairymen's supplies, and was located at Eighteenth and Market streets prior to moving to this address. Because this was built as cold-storage and office facility, it had very few windows and an elaborate brick design was used on the exterior to break up the mass of the building's facade. The large ground-floor windows were once loading docks. This building is credited with having some of the best brick design work in the city, and some of it was copied for use at Coors Field. New additions to this structure were made in 1912 and 1916.

Littleton Creamery was purchased in 1912 by Beatrice Foods. The dairy products for Beatrice Foods were sold under the brand name Meadow Gold which was a name chosen for its products by Beatrice's employees. After 1928

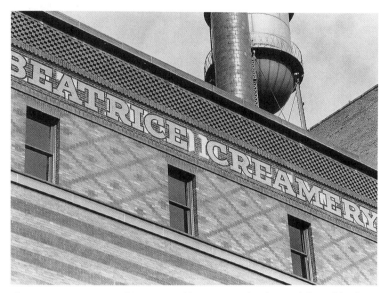

The Ice House, a National Register Building. Notice the diamond-shaped brick-work that was copied at Coors Field. Note also the older sign on the exterior wall reappearing as the newer signs painted over it weather away. — *Randy Brown Photographer*

when Beatrice purchased Windsor Farm Dairy, this building was used for cold storage and butter production. Note the old dairy signage on the front of the original structure and the signs on both sides of the building. Meadow Gold moved its cold storage and butter plant in 1980. The building was reno-vated in 1985 and 1986 by Charles Calloway and Dana Crawford into offices and showrooms.

Walk to Nineteenth Street.

41 UNION PACIFIC FREIGHT HOUSE
1735 Nineteenth Street

This structure was built in 1923 as an inbound freight terminal and offices for the Union Pacific Railroad. It was designed by the office of the Union Pacific chief engineers, and was built as a freestanding structure within a complex of

The Union Pacific Freight House, one of the three historic buildings that were saved on the stadium district property. — *Randy Brown Photographer*

buildings, including a commissary, garage, signal department warehouse, outbound terminal, and automobile dock. At that time, the company handled more than 2,000 rail cars in Denver on an average day. The original loading docks have been removed.

The Union Pacific Freight House is one of three historic properties saved on the stadium district land. Its entryway was considered when designing the main entrance to Coors Field.

42 WYNKOOP PEDESTRIAN WALKWAY

This walkway is the link between the Lower Downtown neighborhood and Coors Field. A public artwork called "Evolution of the Ball" adorns the archway at the end of the mall as a gateway to the stadium. It recalls the "Mizpah"

Coors Field nearing completion — the neighborhood's newest landmark.
— photo by *Suzanne Venino*

arch that once graced the Seventeenth Street entrance to Union Station. The ceramic work has more than 100 different three-dimensional balls worked into the design.

As you complete this tour, we hope you have enjoyed seeing some of Denver's hidden treasures and the parts of the past that have been successfully preserved.

INDEX

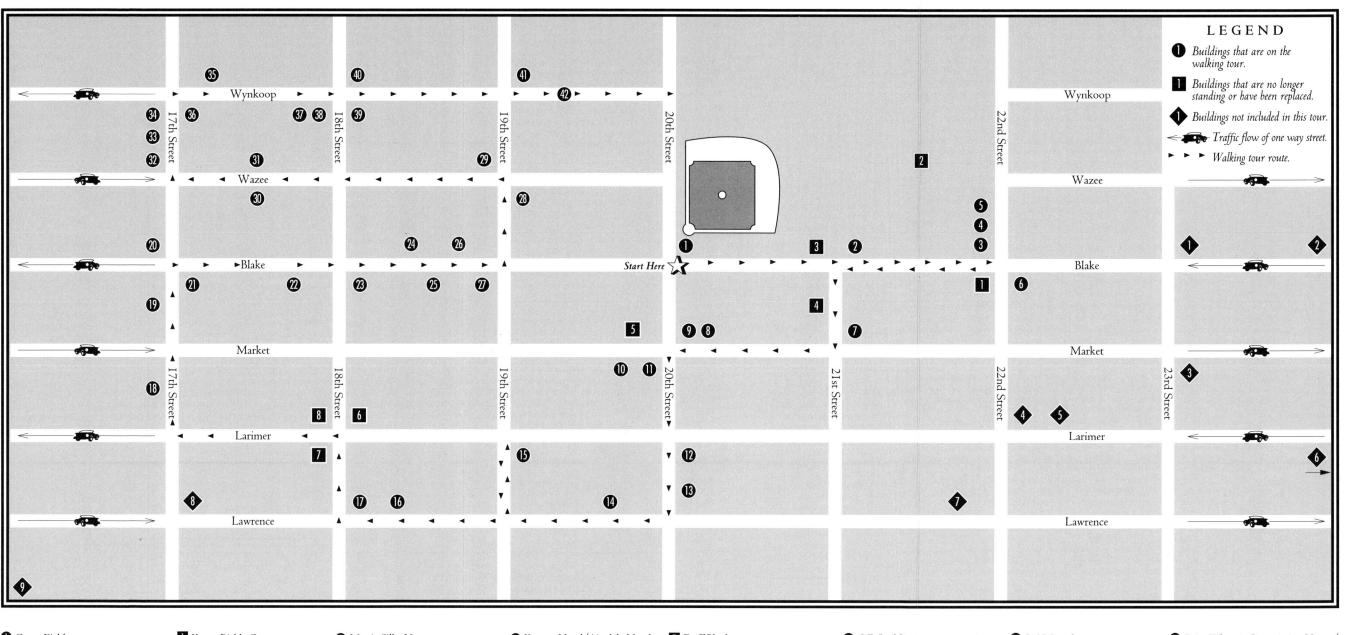

LEGEND

● Buildings that are on the walking tour.

■ Buildings that are no longer standing or have been replaced.

◆ Buildings not included in this tour.

⬅🚗 Traffic flow of one way street.

▶ ▶ ▶ Walking tour route.

① Coors Field
② Diamond Mine Store & Rocky Mountain Baseball Museum
③ Banker's Warehouse Co. Building
④ "The Bottom of the Ninth"
⑤ Transport Service Station
⑥ Kaminsky Barrel Co. Building
❶ McPhee and McGinnity Building
❷ Pacific Express Stable

■1 Kuner Pickle Company
■2 Denver Pacific Depot
■3 Purox Building/ Windsor Farm Dairy Building
■4 Hop Alley
❼ Piggly Wiggly MacMarr
◆3 Timpte Brothers Wagon Co.
■8 American Legion Post/ Cathay Post/Nisei #185

⑨ Mattie Silks House
⑩ House of Mirrors
■5 Lizzie Preston's "House"
⑪ El Chapultepec
◆4 The Thorndyke/Burlington Hotel
◆5 Christopher Columbus Hall/ El Bronco Bar
■6 Sacred Heart Church
⑫ Quaker Hotel

⑬ Kopper Hotel/Airedale Hotel
❼ Ainsworth Building
⑭ Tri-State Buddhist Temple
⑮ Sakura Square
⑯ J.P. Dunn Building
⑰ Denver City Cable Railway Company/Spaghetti Factory
㉑ St. Elmo Hotel
㉒ Windsor Stables Building/Windsor OmniBus & Carriage Co. Stables

■7 Duff Block
■8 Barclay Block
❾ D&F Tower and Tabor Center
⑱ Columbia Hotel
⑲ Market Street Station
⑳ Union Warehouse/Barth Hotel
❽ Gumry Hotel
■6 Windsor Hotel

㉓ G.E. Building
㉔ Firehouse #5
㉕ Crocodilos II
㉖ Windsor Farm Dairy
㉗ F.W. Crocker & Company Steam Cracker Factory/Nabisco Building
㉘ Wazee Exchange
㉙ Beebe & Runyan Building

㉚ S&H Supply
㉛ Hendrie & Bolthoff
㉜ Oxford Hotel
㉝ Oxford Annex
㉞ Struby Estabrook
㉟ Union Depot/Union Station
㊱ Denver City Railway Company Building/Sheridan Heritage

㊲ Spice Whse. & Commission House/ Edward W. Wynkoop Building
㊳ J.S. Brown Mercantile Building
㊴ BDT Building/Atrium Building
㊵ Littleton Creamery/Beatrice Foods/ The Ice House
㊶ Union Station Freight House
㊷ Wynkoop Pedestrian Walkway